"Sonja takes you from the basics to the bold; from the simple to the splendid. Everything you want and need to know about effective signing."

—John Pellegrine
Senior Vice President, Target Stores

"Everyone in retailing realizes the importance of signing. That's why there are so many signs! Unfortunately, few know how to properly use them for their main purpose—as a service to the customer. Sonja's book provides the information necessary to help retailers get the most out of this very critical medium."

—Kenneth A. Banks
Vice President, Marketing Communications, Eckerd Drug Company

"Good merchandise signing (is vitally important because it) is probably the best service available in our struggling 'serviceless economy.' Sonja Larsen knows how to do it and now passes it on in a realistic and practical book. It's fun, too. Get it, read it, and act! You'll improve your signing —and your sales."

—Peter Glen
Marketing Consultant, author of "It's Not My Department!"

"A comprehensive book on effective store signing? An idea so simple only a brilliant mind could conceive of it. A significant contribution to successful retail marketing. Much of the battle for the hearts, minds, and cash of retail shoppers in the 90's will be fought in the arena of visual marketing—selling the customer (who is) in the store. Sonja's new signing book is a significant resource in the battle, regardless of store size or format."

—Tom Holliday
Executive Vice President, RAMA

Signs That Sell

The Handbook of Successful Merchandise Signing

By Sonja Larsen

Published by Insignia Systems, Inc.

Minneapolis, Minnesota, 1991

Printed in the U.S.A.

Published by I N S I G N I A   S Y S T E M S ,   I N C .

10801 Red Circle Drive, Minnetonka, MN 55343

Phone: 1-800-874-4648

Fax: 612-930-8222

Library of Congress Cataloging-in-Publication Data

Larsen, Sonja.

Signs That Sell.

The Handbook of Successful Merchandise Signing, Seventh Edition

ISBN 0-9629666-1-4

ACKNOWLEDGEMENTS

The author wishes to acknowledge her debt
to Karen Singer Gershman and Pat Leahy,
her signing associates for 10 years at Target.
To the people at Insignia Systems, Inc., who recognized the need
and took responsibility for answering that need.
For their support and encouragement—and their suggestions
which almost doubled the size of this book.
To her husband, Stan, her coach
and counselor for 30 years.

Table of Contents

Publisher's Foreword

RETAILERS AND SERVICE PEOPLE have been using signs since trade began—even before the general public was literate. Early signs were carved and painted pieces of folk art—art that illustrated the name of the inn, or the major classification of merchandise to be sold. Three large balls announced the pawn shop. A huge carved fish hung over the fishmonger's shop. Travelers used these early "international symbols" to find the shop they needed. The general public, who couldn't read, could cope.

With the printing press, literacy became more common. Eventually, mandated schooling gave much of the world a literate public. Signing ceased to be folk art and became an art form. Typestyles flourished and dramatic, swooping logos made their appearances. The carriage trade liked scripts and flourishes.

Signing stopped being a "form" and became more of a "function" with contemporary ideas of simplicity. Life's tempo increased. The customer was in a hurry and anxious to get the information—fast. Helvetica type became popular. No frills, no serifs, just simple communication.

Advertising quickly developed into a sophisticated print, and then radio and television form. Meanwhile, signing was slow to evolve. The professionals who agonized over every ad's photograph did not give signs much attention. A beautiful ad could be supported in the store with a handwritten sign—or no sign at all! Even though the business school textbooks had chapters on the effectiveness of signing—it just didn't get strong support from store management. This situation is, like so much in retailing, changing faster today than ever before.

In the last 30 years, retail management techniques have developed dramatically—principally because of computer technology. Price look-up systems (PLU) told retailers exactly what had been sold. That led to better inventory control and closer ties with manufacturers. It helped stores stay in stock and give better customer service. It also allowed store management to "play" with pricing to test customer reaction and then forecast sales and gross margins. The "I wonder what would happen if . . . " ponderings of a store buyer could be put into the computer, with variations, to find out quickly what *could* happen if—this sort of forecasting helped successful retailers survive competitive attacks on their prices and margins.

Technology came to signing too. Just as computer technology promised a new world to marketing people, it promised professional printing and reproduction to sign managers. However, the early technology was complicated—specialists were as necessary to the first sign technologies as they are to today's mainframe computer systems. Technology threatened to overwhelm the task.

But now, with Insignia's Impulse and Stylus Sign Systems, technology has been focused to meet the needs of retailers. After years of market research and customer needs assessment, a Minnesota company, Insignia Systems, has developed products that combine marketplace realities with technology to solve even the most difficult signing problems. The Company realized that nothing was available for the smaller retailer or for the chain store that needed flexibility. Insignia found its niche—and the technology. Advances in software and special application computers were matched with graphic and typography advancements so that professional print quality signs could now be made easily, by the smallest to the largest retailers.

Why This Book

As Insignia Systems executives were assessing the market need for sign-making systems, we discovered that a majority of stores still make signs by hand due to the need for flexibility and fast turnaround. We also discovered that information about signing was primarily anecdotal—store managers knew signs worked, but not exactly how well or why. Insignia's retail customers were not aware of any literature on signing, yet when our executives checked into the research that did exist, we found proof that proper signs improved

sales. There were needs for simple, flexible signing systems, but there was also a need for a book that compiled the sporadic research on signing with the practical experience of a successful retail executive.

Hence, this book. It is aimed at all retailers, large or small, as well as those who create and provide signs as a service. Some references and ideas may not be applicable to your operation, but we have tried to present a range of practical solutions. In many cases we have provided real life examples as thought-starters for you as you develop, change or fine-tune your signing philosophy and efforts.

How to Use This Book

This book is not intended to be read as a novel or even a textbook, from front to back. The chapters are self-contained, to be investigated as you see the need. Some chapters are quite theoretical, others have specific examples and ideas you can use today.

This is a handbook and is meant to be referred to frequently.

This Edition

There will be many ideas and areas that we did not cover in this edition of Signs That Sell. If you would send us your comments and ideas, we will do our best to update this handbook on a regular basis, and will incorporate whatever we learn from you. Our intent is to continue to provide retailers with the best current information in a simple reference book. We will need your help to accomplish our goal.

If you have questions about anything in this book, or are interested in learning more about better merchandising and signage, call us at 1-800-874-4648. One of our merchandising specialists will be glad to help!

—*The Publisher*

Author's Introduction

WHAT IS A FOUR-LETTER WORD THAT BEGINS WITH "S"? Hint: no one wants to take responsibility for it. When it *is* brought to your attention, it is accompanied with the question "Who did *that*?" What am I talking about? A SIGN.

If all this sounds familiar, it is because you have a typical sign process. It may be *your* step-child if you're an independent store owner. If you're part of a store chain, signing can be a distant relative of your advertising chief, your display director or your store manager. In any case, it's a sure bet that signing doesn't get the attention—and loving tender care—that it deserves. Who *does* have responsibility for signs in your business? This is an important question, because signing *is* important, yet the responsibility for signing is usually shared by several people—and typically signing is not anyone's primary job responsibility.

Whoever *is* basically responsible for sign production, another sure bet is that he or she has had it with complaints. (That is one of the caveats of signing: everyone complains. No one ever compliments. Honestly, have you *ever* complimented your sign makers for a good job? It's time you did.)

Repeat: signing *is* important. Signing can increase sales significantly. Research proves it. Ask any buyer who has added a sign to a presentation (with a good price, of course) and watched the increase. It's one of those basics of business that is *so* basic, we neglect it.

If you're an independent store owner, you have probably delegated sign making to the person with the most legible handwriting—in addition to his or her "regular" job. How the signing gets made is a haphazard process with rush requests for "do it yesterday." Being the sign maker, one can feel as if the rest of the organization is, if not working *against* you, at least not working *with* you.

The process of getting *all* the signs necessary to do business, and getting them *right* and *on time* represents a major logistical challenge to the smaller retailer. Outside resources aren't geared to the speed of change that is demanded by the retail business. Inside resources are limited—a small operation can't

Who gets called when the ad signs aren't up on time? Or does anybody care?

afford to have a person dedicated solely to sign making. Responsibilities for signs are usually divided according to who has free time—and the results are usually haphazard.

In a chain-store operation, the situation simply gets more complicated. No matter what your store size, it's time for a review of your signing process. First, what is your current sign program costing you? Are you still operating, with 40 stores, the same as when you had four? Or operating four stores the same way as when you had only one? Is your signing in the age

of technology or are you still using primitive forms of hand printing? What do your store managers and department managers say about your signing programs—that's printable? Are sale signs tied into your advertising programs or do they have a shelf life of their own?

To help you track responsibility, just answer this question. Who gets called when the ad signs aren't up on time? Or does anybody care?

As you know, display directors think signs are the awful clutter that intrudes on their beautiful presentations and "arrangements." No display director (well, almost no one) ever incorporates a sign into a presentation design. It comes after. Way after. Possibly never. To be taken down as soon as possible.

Now let's talk about the buyers. After spending hours agonizing about assortments, new trends, and special sales efforts—they throw their ad request forms over the transom and forget to request a sign until the day the ad breaks, or the day they get a call from some store manager, asking about some new merchandise. Signing is perpetually at the bottom of their "To Do" list.

Advertising directors have their hands full with the last-minute ads and changes that run rampant in retail businesses. It's hard to keep track of the signs that must coordinate with the ads, but it's possible. However, how much clout does the ad director have with store personnel (the ones who have to put the sign *up* and take it *down* on time) and who report to a store manager?

There's the second rub. Implementation. Once you know who is responsible, *in the stores,* for signs—how do you know if that person is doing a good job? Is there any formal review process? Is there any simple list of which signs should be up this week, that

Customers need signs!

- **to identify advertised merchandise**
- **to explain hidden benefits**
- **to indicate value and price**
- **to highlight new trends**
- **to explain the difference between look-alike products**
- **to be reminded to purchase products they may need with this purchase**
- **to know where to find what they are looking for**
- **to understand your important policies, such as returns**

You need signs!

- **to "trade up" a customer to a better-margin product**
- **to suggestion-sell other products (cross merchandising)**
- **to increase impulse purchases**
- **to convince the customer of his or her need for any one product!**

managers could carry around and check as they visit stores? Is anyone *rewarded* for having the proper signs up? And having last week's signs taken down? Is anyone *punished* for doing a bad sign job? (If you really want to check your performance, visit a store the day after a minor seasonal event, such as Valentine's Day or St. Patrick's Day— just count how many signs still refer to what is now very old news.)

How about the *quantity* of signs? Is it up to the individual department manager? If so, then if one manager is bullish on signs, that department has lots. If another manager isn't interested, that department has almost no signs. Should it be up to the individual? (Ever had an aggressive new assistant overwhelm a department with signs? It seems to be part of the on-the-job-training program.) Do your people have guidelines?

A smaller store can have a simple set of guidelines. A large chain usually has a huge sign manual with directions to the stores about what kinds of signs to expect and where to put each one. In either case, when was it reviewed by anybody? It can be an embarrassing experience to find references to signholders that no longer exist. Or references to sales events that you no longer put on your calendar. (Is your "Electronics Sale" still signed as a "Sound Sale"? It has happened.)

I've asked a lot of questions, all of which you should be asking yourself and every key person in your organization. Remember, what gets *inspected* is what gets *respected*. You need to inspect—the who, the what, the where, the how and the when of your current sign program—and what it all costs.

The purpose of a sign is primarily *service to the customer*. So, in this era of revived interest in (and customer demand for) service, there should be a revived interest in signing.

When your signs do one or more of the above, they increase sales. If they don't do any of the above, why are they there? Does your sign policy have any guidelines for making a judgment on signing content? It should.

Who is the czar of signing in your operation? Who is the person who says, "We really need a sign here," or alternatively,

---

It is much easier (and cheaper) to get your current customers to spend a few more dollars with you than it is to get new customers to come to your store.

"That's a bad sign idea and it's NOT going into our store."? Is your sign maker an implementer—someone who processes all signs just as fast as possible, no matter what the copy says? Or is your sign maker a MANAGER, who refuses to process dumb signs, and who teaches everyone else in your store the difference? Get yourself a manager who knows how he or she can influence store sales and loves the opportunity

I warn you, sign making is

an absolutely thankless responsibility. No one ever notices a sign until something goes wrong—and things do go wrong. Under normal store conditions, the person in charge needs steady nerves, good spelling, thick skin and a source of psychological satisfaction separate from the job.

Your challenge is to change your organization and improve its operations to be better than "normal store conditions." Then you will have signing that gets respect. You will have signing that customers recognize as good service. You will enjoy increased sales, with a minimum of expense.

Consider this: it is much easier (and cheaper) to get your *current* customers to spend a few more dollars with you, than it is to get *new* customers to come to your store. Of course you need new customers. But if your current customers are happy, their word of mouth advertising for you is priceless. If you will take your sign program seriously, you will be able to increase your average transaction, you will satisfy more customers—and have fewer people walk out your doors without buying anything.

Genius is in the details. Selling success is in the signing!

Back to Basics

We live in perilous times. Events across the globe can cause customers to slow—if not stop—spending. Successful manufacturing operations in other countries can cause swift regional recessions in ours. The proliferation of discount chain stores brings more than one power marketer to your trade area. Meanwhile, more and more stores are carrying the same branded products! How can a smaller, independent retailer survive? By going back to the basics and doing them better. When you're battered and bruised from new competition and the customers' pressure for more value, you are tempted to "do something different." You are tempted to add a few frills, add a new promotional campaign, add new lines of merchandise—in short, grasp at promises. It is far better to go back to the foundation of good retailing and mine the

Signing is the one sales promotion effort which is guaranteed to get results.

basics for opportunities. You have probably forgotten more basic opportunities than you will ever find in "blue sky" new ideas!

Consider this: a research study done in *1974,* published in the *Journal of Marketing Research,* concluded that a *special display* sold more than an in-store price reduction without a sign, and sold *more than merchandise advertised in a newspaper ad* without a sign. Yet, how many hours do you spend working on your newspaper advertising, forgetting entirely about your in-store signing potential?

More research was done in the 1980's, supporting the in-store research of 1974. Conclusions stayed the same. Displays with signing work exceptionally well. Now there is research which clearly defines the benefits of *printed* signs versus *handwritten!* Yet, where is signing on the average retailer's "To Do" list? Too close to the bottom for any retailer's serious attention. That is wrong.

Every retailer today is experiencing unprecedented pressures on profits. Every square foot of store space must perform better in order to survive, let alone thrive. Let's assume you have ruthlessly pared your assortments and refined your inventory to improve turnover and gross margins. You may not be able to increase your advertising budget. You can't afford a total-store refixturing or redecoration. You may not be able to afford more good salespeople. But you *can* rejuvenate your signing program.

Signing is the one sales promotion effort which is guaranteed to get results (check the research); at the same time signing is the lowest-cost strategy available! Perhaps that's why signs don't get any respect. They're too obvious. They're too basic.

Signing is the one sales promotion effort which can, *at low cost,* significantly change your store image. Signing can make the customer feel smart. Signing can make the customer believe that he or she has made the right purchase decision. Signing can drive your competition crazy, as you change pricing strategies and prices. While a large discount chain may be tied into national promotions and national or regional pricing, small chains and independents are more able to change prices "on a dime." Signing can be guerrilla warfare against the giants.

Signing is an important

> *Signing is the one sales promotion effort which can, at low cost, significantly change your store image.*

part of the customers' perception of value in your store. Thus, if your signs are hand-printed and look cheap, you devalue the product in the eyes of the consumer. If your signs are neat, printed and include feature benefits, you enhance the value of the product. To the customer, the higher the perceived value, and the lower the price—the bigger the bargain. And the smarter the customer!

As you go through this book, you will find research that will surprise you. You will find "Retailing 101" principles that you originally read years ago and have half-forgotten. You may find that you have been operating with priorities well-planned and executed years ago—and that now, today's changing values, demographics or technology have made those priorities obsolete.

You should know that technology has caught up with your signing needs. Today, your store can have printed signs as quickly and as easily as you once had handwritten signs. Your store personnel can create timely signs—change displays with the arrival of new merchandise—react to competition—in minutes.

Take today's technology—and mix it well with the traditional, basic rules of good in-store presentation. Then put "Signing" at the top of your TO DO's for the 90's! ◆

1. Signs Do Sell—Research Proves It

EVERY MERCHANDISER KNOWS THAT SIGNS WORK; every good merchandiser knows how to forecast sales based on good signing and pricing. Unfortunately, most of what we know about signs is anecdotal—corporate folklore passed on from buyer to buyer. This situation exists because many of the earlier efforts to formalize information about signing were led by trade associations and the information stayed industry-specific. When large retailers organized their own research, they considered the results proprietary. Today there is a small body of research on signing which has been reported in retail publications. There is little, if any, conflict between the research findings. A common conclusion: price-benefit signing increases sales. "How much" seems to depend upon the kind of store and merchandise offered. For this book, the author selected excerpts from three different research studies. Each used well-planned and controlled research techniques; each based the results on different merchandise and store types.

Skaggs Research

The introduction to the Skaggs Institute research says it all:

"Since the introduction of the self-service concept in retailing, the application of point-of-purchase (POP) sales promotion aids has increased greatly among retailers. One major component of the POP promotional mix is the use of in-store POP signs. However, the effectiveness of POP signing is still much debated, and academic research examining its causal effect on sales is noticeably lacking. Retailers are faced with the controversial questions of whether or not to use signs, which type of message content to include on signs (i.e., price only or benefit statements), and whether to use signs for sale items only, or also for items at regular price.

The purpose of this paper is to report a field study that focused on these questions."

The products which were field tested were "high involvement" rather than commodity items. They were: bath towels, pantyhose, ladies' slacks, men's dress slacks, men's jeans and men's shirts.

Signs sell.
Good *signs sell more.*

Summary Results

"The major research objective . . . was to examine the sales effectiveness of three signing conditions: no sign, price-only sign, and benefit sign, at regular and sale prices. A randomized balanced block design was used to rotate the six conditions for the products in three outlets of a national department store chain. The results indicate that at a regular price, a benefit sign should be the only type of sign used, while *at a sale price, both a price-only and a price-plus-benefit sign will increase sales over a no-sign condition, with price-plus-benefit signing being the most effective.*"

In an article in *RAMA Digest*, Winter 1991, Dr. K. Patrick Kelly explained the results of this research further:

"Marking down the items caused the most significant differences to show up. At sale price, the price-only sign resulted in a 24% sales increase, but the benefit sign stimulated *49% more sales than having no sign.*[1]

So, a benefit sign is actually more effective than a price-only sign in moving sale-priced merchandise."

In the first Skaggs study, 33 products were monitored with and without signs. The average overall daily sales rate among the 33 products tested *increased 26% through the use of descriptive signs.*

All three studies conducted by researchers in the Skaggs Institute of Retail Management show undeniably (Dr. Kelly's term) that price-plus-benefit signs are vital sales tools: they generate the greatest increases in sales rates over the other methods tested.

For further information about these studies, contact Dr. Kelly at (313) 577-4536, or Director Robison, Skaggs Institute of Retail Management, Brigham Young University, 480 TNRB, Provo, UT 84602.

[1] "Sales Effects of Point-of-Purchase In-Store Signing" by McKinnon, Kelly and Robison, Skaggs Institute of Retail Management, Brigham Young University, Provo, Utah. Published in *Journal of Retailing,* Summer 1981.

Mueller Research Study

This study, done for the hardware industry, showed how to achieve significant sales increases—numbers made especially dramatic when one sees the mundane products involved: water sealant, all-purpose lubricants, trash cans, light bulbs, extension cords, toilet seats. The research utilized a mixture of signing and merchandising techniques.[2]

SUMMARY FINDINGS FROM THE MUELLER MERCHANDISING STUDY

MERCHANDISING TECHNIQUES	PRODUCTS TESTED	SALES INCREASE
Power displays with feature/benefit and price sign	Water Sealant/all-purpose lubricants	540%
Shared Endcap		
• With feature/benefit/price sign	Water Sealant	229%
• With price only sign	Water Sealant	131%
• With feature/benefit sign only	Water Sealant	112%
• With no sign	Water Sealant	112%
Drive Aisle Stack Display	30-gallon trash cans	79%
Cross-Merchandising	50′ extension cord w/string trimmers	67%
Dump Bin Display	6′ household extension cord	43%
Counter Display	All-purpose lubricant	40%
Price signs (reg. price) displayed on non-impulse item	Toilet seats	25%

[2] "Merchandising to Maximize Sales Productivity" conducted by The Farnsworth Group, Inc., and published by The Russell R. Mueller Retail Hardware Research Foundation in November 1989. (Copies are available from the Foundation, 5822 W. 74th St., Indianapolis, IN 46278. Write or FAX 317-290-0378 for purchasing information.)

LEK Partnership Research

The primary objective of the LEK market research study was to measure the impact of machine-printed signs on sales, compared to the impact of handwritten signs. Basic commodities, such as branded rice, made up a collection of 124 products in the test, conducted in supermarkets and convenience stores in Boston and Los Angeles. Results: [3]

There was a 56% sales increase on merchandise featured with machine-printed signs instead of handwritten signs. The 56% is an average sales increase experienced by both supermarkets and convenience stores. For machine-printed signs compared to no signs, increases averaged 165%.

For supermarkets, machine-printed signs caused 59% higher sales than handwritten signs and 202% higher sales than no signs. For convenience stores, machine-printed signs increased sales by 50% over handwritten signs and 53% over no signs. (Customers appear to shop convenience stores with more specific items in mind. Since impulse purchases are less likely, the sales increase with machine-printed signs was lower in convenience stores than grocery stores.)

Because the sales impact of signs was measured on a product basis, the impact on overall stores sales will necessarily differ. The LEK test demonstrates the effectiveness of machine-printed signs in focusing the consumers' attention on the products that retailers most want to sell.

The sales impact of signs increased with sign size. Test results indicated that larger signs (5½ x 7″) are more powerful than smaller signs (3½ x 5½″) in increasing sales. Probably because they are more successful in capturing the customers' attention.

There you have it. Fascinating proof of the effectiveness of a good sign program. ◆

SUMMARY FINDINGS OF THE LEK PARTNERSHIP STUDY

	SALES INCREASE IN SUPERMARKETS	SALES INCREASE IN CONVENIENCE STORES
Machine-printed signs versus no signs	202%	53%
Machine-printed signs versus handwritten signs	59%	50%

---

[3] "Sales Impact of Signs" by The LEK Partnership, Boston, MA, 1990.

2. Signing Basics

IN ORDER TO KEEP A CONSISTENT LOOK within a store, the size of the signs needs to be disciplined. You might want to limit signs on gondola runs to small sizes, because the customer needs space to take the item off the shelf. End-cap signs can be larger—but how large? Decide for yourself, just make sure they are all the same size. Selecting the proper sizes for your store will be determined by the quantity and quality of your merchandise and your price image. Here are the standard sizes:

> $2^1/4$ x $3^5/8$ inches
> $3^1/2$ x $5^1/2$ inches
> $5^1/2$ x 7 inches (most popular size)
> 7 x 11 inches
> 11 x 14 inches (half sheet)
> 22 x 14 inches
> 22 x 28 inches (full sheet or poster size)

Signholders come in these standard sizes. If you always use sign cards of at least 7.5 mil thickness for your signs, you will have a minimum standard of quality and durability (it will resist curling) that not only will keep the sign in the holder, but can be used without a holder in some applications.

Sign Sizes

Stores with hand-printed signs are limited to larger sizes because of the difficulty of presenting enough information in hand-print. Look at how the same information can be used in several small sizes, with type.

How many of the larger-size signs should you have in your store? Again, it depends. "Poster" sizes usually need a large, floor-stand signholder. This sign and its stand can impede traffic flow unless it's positioned perfectly. It can overwhelm a small display. Be very careful and limit your use of these signs to major storewide announcements, with few exceptions.

SPECIAL

Heet ANTI-FREEZE

- Fuel system dryer
- Takes the water out
- 12-ounce size

Reg. 59¢

2/.90

CLEARANCE

GAS LINE ANTI-FREEZE

Reg. 59¢
12-oz. size

- Fuel system dryer
- Takes the water out
- While supplies last

2/.90

CLEARANCE

GAS LINE ANTI-FREEZE

Reg. 59¢
12-oz. size

- Fuel system dryer
- Takes the water out
- While supplies last

2/.90

The next largest sizes, 22 x 14″ and 11 x 14″ can hold a significant list of items—battery sizes and prices, for instance. One sign may be preferable to a jungle of small signs. You need to analyze your presentation and try it several ways. You'll see what's best. These size signs can also be used for very special price/value offerings.

Typefaces and Typestyles

As a general rule, hardlines products can tolerate a stronger, more bold typeface, and apparel and higher-price products will look best in a lighter, less bold typeface.

Look at these different signs for different products. These signs look appropriate to the products they are promoting.

TORO MOWER

● **Self-propelled**
● **21″ cut**
● **Model #21-4270**

Reg. $289

$199

27.95

Pendleton Shirts

● Real wool for real warmth
● Classic plaids in red or green
● Youth sizes 14 - 20, adult sizes S, M, L, & XL

Here is a potential problem. If these "Satin Jackets" are satin warm-up jackets in the sportswear department, then the typeface is appropriate. If these are women's satin jackets, the typeface is too bold and masculine. The width of the type needs to be made smaller.

$69.00

Satin Jacket

● Nylon shell
● Polyester fiberfill
● Snap front closures

This enhances the value of the satin jackets and looks right in a women's department.

$69.00

Satin Jacket

● Nylon shell
● Polyester fiberfill
● Snap front closures

Another consideration is the type style. Little "ends" to lettering are called serifs. Here are examples of a serif type—very classic:

Athletic Shoes

for the whole family

New Balance Swifts	$38.95
Nike Sportsters	$33.95
Puma Soccer Shoes	$41.95
Reebok Workouts	$29.95
Converse Youth	$32.95
L.A. Gear Malibu	$39.95
El Tigrè Clawtracks	$33.00
Converse All-Star	$25.90
gic"	$69.95
dan	$97.50
ourt	$67.00
amp	$72.50

124.00

"The Pump" by Reebok

- Pump air into the lining for custom fit
- Gridded sole pattern for traction
- Sizes 8 to 13

Here are examples of sans-serif typefaces.

A Helvetica style typeface is preferred by many department and discount stores because it has a light, medium and bold face that looks good with soft-lines or hardlines, depending upon the strength of the letters.

SPECIAL

Heet ANTI-FREEZE

- Fuel system dryer
- Takes the water out
- 12-ounce size

Reg. 59¢

2/.90

Unadvertised
Special

30%

off marked price

2.49

Oscar Mayer Bacon

- Healthier! Lower salt, less fat
- One-pound package
- Second package half-price

Special typefaces usually have limitations—this one, for instance, looks like a grocery store; it does not come in a lighter face.

It does give you all the benefits of type quality, and the ability to add product selling points. It has a friendly feeling.

A few years ago the decision about type was an expensive decision. Today, it can be as simple as a few quick key strokes on a sign system keyboard.

Layout

The arrangement of copy, price and sometimes illustration, creates a "layout." Many stores have basic formats that give all signs a common look—it's then easier for the customer to read all the signs. Sign layouts are

CANDY BARS
3/1^{00}
SNICKERS, M & M's, HERSHEY'S

based on customers' reading habits and are designed to be read as quickly and as easily as possible.

Here's how a sign would look if all the type were set the same size:

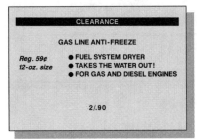

Obviously, nothing stands out, so it is confusing to read. Nothing is dominant and eye-catching. At right we see what a layout can do.

Normally, the price is the feature. It is set in the largest-size type. There's no reason not to. As the merchandise itself (supported by the sign) conveys

CLEARANCE

GAS LINE ANTI-FREEZE

Reg. 59¢
12-oz. size

● Fuel system dryer
● Takes the water out
● While supplies last

2/.90

"Tough as the game ..."

Rugby Shirts

● 100% cotton
● Wrinkle resistant
● Machine washable
● Many colors, styles
● Size S, M, L, and XL

29.50

Regular $39.50

a customer's first question ("What is it?") the sign should immediately answer the second question—"How much is it?"

Our language is read left to right, top to bottom. Therefore, a layout that uses our typical reading pattern is most familiar to us and is most easily read.

The sign on the right has everything centered. This can be an elegant look, but use it with care. It works best on larger-size signs with very simple copy. The sign below, in an outline sort of form, is easier to read.

Here Comes Winter

SALE

Ladies'
Multi-color, All wool
Sweaters
One size fits most
While available

21.00

Holiday Sale!

SEPARATES

● Resist wrinkles
● Perfect for travel
● 55% linen, 45% polyester

Jackets $98   **Pants $65**

Our eyes tend to look first at a spot slightly above the center of a sign. It is the "hot spot" where you should put your headline or most important message other than price. Sometimes put your price there!

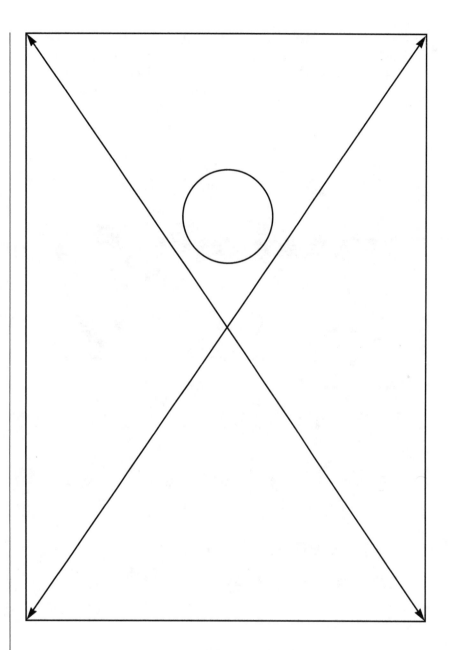

The principles of sign layout are similar to advertising layout. You need to consider:

Balance—the use of white space between elements, and balancing the elements themselves to avoid lopsided looking signs. Note how this sign is almost divided in half, with a dominant price on top, separated by a single bar, to the copy below. An excellent example of balance.

21.95

Northland® Hockey Sticks

☞ 2-ply fiberglass blade reinforcement

☞ SuperFlex shaft for accurate shots

☞ Right or Left, Lies 5 and 6

Proportion—type sizes shouldn't be too diverse. Type sizes should relate to each other on the same sign. There should be a limit to type size per sign size. Don't make type sizes too overwhelming. A good example: Notice that the word "SALE" and the price are almost the same type size. The price at the bottom gives proportion to the headline.

BATTERY

SALE

- Cadmium-Plus technology
- 575 cold-cranking amps
- Maintenance-free
- Streamlined size
- 60-month warranty
- Fits all cars and pick-ups

42.95

Dominance—something should stand out. Ideally, there should be one thing dominant, one thing sub-dominant, and all the rest should be tertiary and equal. Simplicity—nothing can beat simple, elegant communication. Don't confuse the copy with a lot of curlicues or fancy borders. White space is necessary. Don't mix different typefaces on one sign. It's more difficult to read. Use reverse type sparingly, and if possible, for only one or two words.

SPECIAL

Heet ANTI-FREEZE

- Fuel system dryer
- Takes the water out
- 12-ounce size

Reg. 59¢

2/.90

CLEARANCE

GAS LINE ANTI-FREEZE

Reg. 59¢
12-oz. size

- Fuel system dryer
- Takes the water out
- While supplies last

2/.90

Once you have an idea of what your store needs, you can select formats or sign guidelines, with character limits and automatic type sizes, and the rest is a simple matter. Sign forms can look like this. ◆

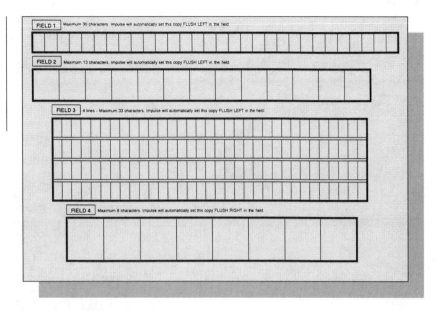

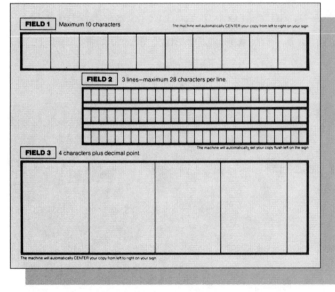

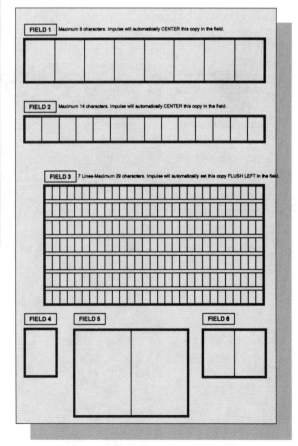

3. Signing for Impulse Purchases: More Sales and Profits

ADVERTISING CREATIVE DIRECTORS have staked their reputations on a misquote from Chinese history: "A picture is worth a thousand words." Actually, the original statement translates roughly but more accurately to mean: one look is worth a thousand words. That is, better to see for yourself than depend on the stories and oral reports of others. Most retailers would appreciate that!

Retail executives have modified that quote to: "A store visit is worth a hundred pictures." There is nothing like actually being in a store to experience its merchandising and to feel the vigor of its promotional efforts.

Every endcap has powerful potential. Plan ahead—to promote what the customer wants most—each month or even each weekend. "Shoot while the ducks are flying" is the strategy to increase sales.

If I had to choose three stores as a sort of MBA in merchandising, I would recommend these three as well worth the store visit: Stew Leonard's in Norwalk, Connecticut, a Target store in your neighborhood and Byerly's grocery store in St. Louis Park, a suburb of Minneapolis.

Stew Leonard's

Stew Leonard's started as a dairy store and has expanded in all directions and to about 800 items (versus the average supermarket's 25,000!). They have promotional platforms which are monitored constantly. If any platform merchandise is not performing according to projections, *it is taken down immediately* and restocked with another item.

The store has a "race track" aisle which takes you past every item and guides you to a generous amount of checkouts. It's not only very easy to shop, it's entertaining! The promotional gimmicks at Stew Leonard's are famous: the mechanical cows, the security person dressed like a movie-lot

> *"A store visit is worth a hundred pictures."*

sheriff, a petting zoo for kids, thousands of pictures and greetings from customers and pictures of employees smiling. No words, no photographs, no videotape can capture the energy of this store. You simply have to experience it, and talk to the employees and customers, in order to grasp the enthusiasm the total effort generates. And wish for more of it in your store!

Target

For years, the Target organization has maintained a disciplined program of endcap and checkout promotions. A single item endcap! Signed with product benefits and price. It is a classic, clean, dominant presentation—endcap after endcap on the main aisle. The endcaps are

changed regularly with emphasis on seasonal merchandise. The result is that the store looks like it *has* plenty of merchandise—when the customer wants it—and at a great price.

Target has a philosophy of dominance—looking dominant via displays, groupings of merchandise, and piling the merchandise onto promotional bases at peak periods. Anyone who has seen Target's mountain of notebook paper during back-to-school, will understand.

Again, a visit is worth a plane ticket. Only an on-site visit will give you the details of cleanliness—the shining floors that are probably cleaner than your kitchen's floor—the crisp decor and disciplined presentations. There is an orderliness to a Target store that helps the customer feel at home—at ease to look for the items he or she wants, and make a purchase with confidence. Every effort is made in the signing to make it easier for the customer to find what he or she is looking for. Even overhead "airport" style signing is used to give directions to various departments.

Target's planning is another part of its genius. Promotional items are located in the logical department or on a nearby end-aisle. You won't find Windex on sale in the curtain department or lingerie! There's a place for everything and everything is in its place. Department locations are planned so that there is a natural flow from one to another—no sharp or jarring adjacencies. You have to walk through it (more than once) to understand the care that is taken with every detail.

Byerly's

Byerly's is listed in the yellow pages under "Grocers" but that hardly describes the experience of this upscale food operation. It has become a tourist attraction! I know several executives who make a Byerly's stop whenever they're entertaining foreign guests. First-time visitors are awed by the carpeting and the chandeliers in the frozen food section, and by the adjacent shops, including a very expensive gift shop which carries top names in crystal as well as fine antiques.

Regular customers are pleased with the assortments —everything from paper towels to caviar. One of the unusual things you might see in the parking lot: people eating and reading the paper in their car. (Byerly's has a deli of excellence, as well as a salad bar.) If you wish to eat in more comfort, they have a restaurant. Byerly's also has a flower market, post office, demonstration kitchen for cooking classes, a special card shop, candy store, yogurt stand, live trout in a tank in their meat department, a newspaper stand with national newspapers, video rentals, unbelievable "home-baked" pies from their bakery, and an adjoining liquor store with an excellent wine selection. They have a service desk for fast check-cashing and the details of buying stamps or mailing items. What more could they offer in service? They're open 24 hours a day!

You have to see the store to understand their gentle way with merchandising and signing. All signs are neatly printed . . . unusual for grocery stores. Their coffee and tea department features a large section of decaffeinated brands, but also coffeemakers, espresso makers, filters and spoons that hold loose tea. Suggestion selling in

the meat area includes timely recipes and meal planning (they have an on-staff home economist). Breads are always part of the cheese presentation. They have regular sampling days, and a special display of all new products being introduced. You will find Swedish Pearl sugar and lutefisk at Christmastime, to satisfy the demands of the local Scandinavian population. You'll also find an equally sensitive assortment of ethnic foods for the Jewish, Oriental and Hispanic audiences.

Byerly's fresh produce department was once rated as a "good place for upscale singles to meet" and became a meeting place. It does all this with printed signs, in-store specials and regular sampling efforts, but doesn't forget dump bins, end-cap promotions and in-store sales.

There you have it—three very successful, very diverse strategies. Guaranteed to be an exciting and educational store tour. Make the trip!

There is nothing really mysterious about what these stores are up to. They have simply taken the basic rules of merchandising and molded them into a unique retail image.

Organize the Gondola to Maximize Gross Margin

With the pressure on shelf space in a typical store today, placing each product is critical. Professionals use a "grid" to begin their planning. Sometimes that grid is on a computer which can automatically estimate the plan's total profitability—when you program in each item's margin and rate of sale. A hand-made grid can guide you to put the most product in place, with the highest margin

merchandise in the best place. Even the most rudimentary planning will pay off in plus sales. It is absolutely necessary in order to plan a sign program which can maximize your sales.

Large chains will use actual merchandise to create a gondola presentation, then photograph it or sketch a diagram to create a "planogram." You can sketch your own—or your vendors may have support help for this effort. Ask them. (When you are planning what to place where, think beyond the simple

problem of size and bulk of the product.)

• 1. Organize merchandise *vertically*—it's easier on the customer. Organize merchandise by color, and work the colors vertically. Organize packaged goods vertically with smaller-sizes on top, larger on shelves below.

• 2. Put your profit-makers at eye level.

• 3. Put slower-moving merchandise at lower levels.

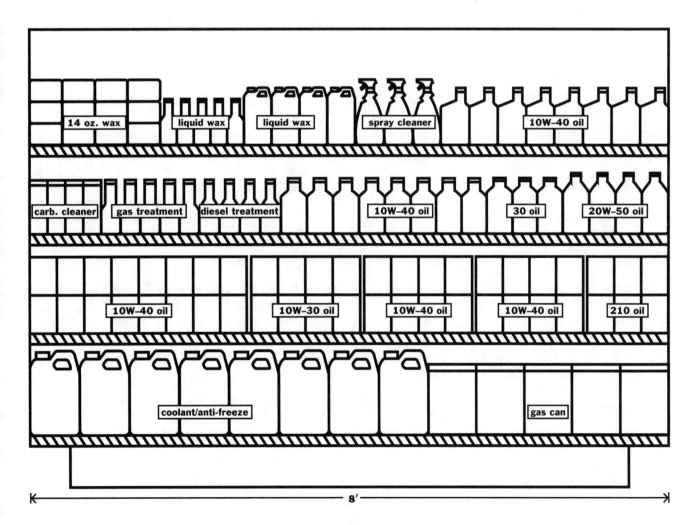

• 4. Try to match the amount of merchandise on the shelf to the demand, according to your replenishment schedule.

• 5. Put your private label next to the brand it relates to—and sign both with benefits and price.

• 6. Make sure all your shelves are equal depth, or that the top shelves are narrower than the bottom shelves.

• 7. Always plan your signs as you plan your merchandise. Always have a plan to promote your best values, your highest margin product, any good/better/best assortments.

When you are planning gondolas, make sure that you think in terms of *aisles* as departments, not the individual gondolas. It is called cross-aisle merchandising. Both sides of the aisle become one department and your presentation looks more dominant to the customer. The customer doesn't have to walk entirely around a gondola to look for everything in your selection—it's on both sides of one aisle!

This arrangement makes it easier for you to sign departmentally, too. And to use the wall at the end aisle for larger items and the opportunity to finish the organization of related items.

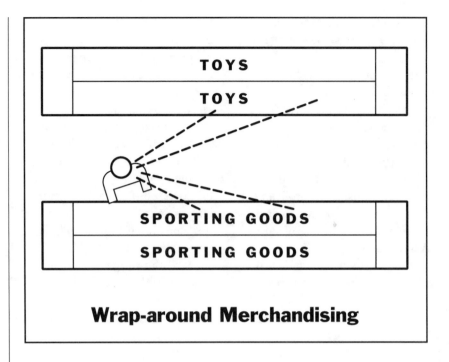

Wrap-around Merchandising

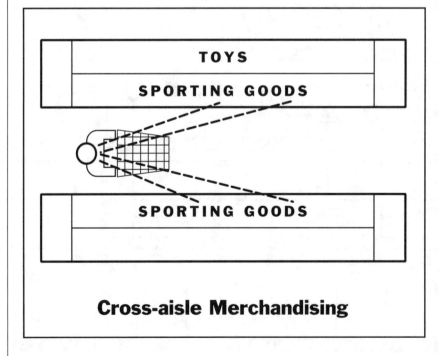

Cross-aisle Merchandising

PLANOGRAM FOR PREGO

PASTA	Extra Chunky 14 oz.		Prego Base 14 oz.		TOMATO PASTE
	Prego No Salt 30 oz.	Extra Chunky Sausage/G.P. 30 oz.	Prego Base 48 oz.		
	Extra Chunky Mushroom/Extra Spice 30 oz.	Extra Chunky Garden Combo 30 oz.	Prego Tomato/Basil 30 oz.	Prego Three Cheese 30 oz.	
	Extra Chunky Mushroom/Green Pepper 30 oz.	Extra Chunky Mushroom/Onion 30 oz.	Prego Onion/Garlic 30 oz.	Prego Regular 30 oz.	
	Extra Chunky Mushroom/Tomato 30 oz.	Extra Chunky Mushroom/Onion 30 oz.	Prego Meat 30 oz.	Prego Mushroom 30 oz.	

Some planograms can be illustrated very simply and easily.

Plan Your Endcaps to Maximize Sales

Endcaps are the ends of each gondola or aisle. The ends facing the main aisles should never be used as permanent displays—they have more important work! In my experience, the simple movement of product from aisle to endcap with nothing else to enhance it—not even a sign—will at least double sales, possibly triple them. The Russell R. Mueller Retail Hardware Research Foundation study on product movement using real-life research in stores, proved that endcap displays (with proper signing) can force sales up to eight times the regular rate—and these were not commodity products!

The three key ingredients to empowering endcaps are:

• Timely selection of the product itself.

• Proper signing to present value—that is, the features and benefits, rather than simply the price.

• Single product or single-idea dominance.

With the above three elements in mind, what should you be using as priorities for your precious endcap space?

Endcap tip #1: Give priority to seasonal merchandise

Here is your opportunity to look new, to enhance your image and to give your seasonal product top exposure to high traffic in your store. When you have only a few months to sell any item, make that selling as high-performance as you can. Seasonal product is usually somewhat impulse, so get it out where it can be seen.

Small stores, no matter how cramped for space, should devote extra time to their planning efforts on the gondola runs in order to free up as many end caps as possible for seasonal presentation. Of course, one-item endcaps are best, but allied products are effective, especially in seasonal presentations.

Because seasonal product is not purchased frequently, the selling benefits of the product are very important. Feature/price signs will be especially effective in increasing sales.

Endcap tip #2: Tell them what's new

Use endcaps to test new products and get an idea of customer acceptance before you plan them into your regular assortment. It will help you determine how much product you need to shelve. It will help you decide how many facings you need, and which "flavor," color, etc., should be included in your regular stock.

Having endcaps free from regular stock allows you to do this testing and also gives your customers the news, fast. It also makes your entire department look fresher and newsier.

Simple price signing is counter-productive here. You need clearly presented product benefits to introduce any new item. Price alone isn't enough to be effective.

Endcap tip #3: Show your commodity dominance

Here is where you present a dominant block of one item and sign it with an aggressive price. Here is where you present a *brand name*—Pampers, Pennzoil, Gitano—and an advertised price. Here is where you present a *timely commodity,* such as small batteries during the Christmas season, with a good but not margin-killing price.

If you have a strong private label program, consider a two-product display, with vertical presentation of the brand and your private label. Sign each side, explaining the product benefits of both and making the price comparison easy for the customer. Here is a good opportunity to test the acceptance of your private label at various prices versus the name brand.

The three key ingredients to empowering endcaps are:

• Timely selection of the product itself.

• Proper signing to present value— that is, the features and benefits, rather than simply the price.

• Single product or single-idea dominance.

Endcap tip #4: Use the rear endcaps for clearance

You may want to use main-aisle endcaps for clearance during a peak clearance month, or just after a peak selling period like Christmas when you have Christmas wrap and cards to get rid of fast. But on a day-to-day basis, you will have better use for main aisle endcaps than clearance. You can teach your customers that clearance is on the back. Or you can use back endcaps for manufacturer displays that are permanent or semi-permanent.

Endcap tip #5: Remind them of what they need, when they need it

Consider when the customer may be coming in for a "destination" purchase—paint, rollers or ladder for instance. Use the endcap to be a combination of service-reminders of what else is needed, and impulse purchases. Organize an endcap display of all the small products (you don't need to put brushes and paint rollers here) needed to complete a paint job: masking tape, thinner, paint remover, tools, sandpaper.

Look for other "project" opportunities in the do-it-yourself area and in the areas of cooking, baking, entertaining, etc. (How many women have bought a turkey, taken it home and stuffed it, only to discover that they don't have a pan big enough to hold it? Too many!) Check your calendar for seasonal opportunities. Try a pre-Thanksgiving display of roasting pans, basters, foil and baking bags. When you have organized your presentation, use shelf-talkers to present the features/benefits of each product.

Look for Opportunities to Cross-merchandise

Cross-merchandising is simply putting product in more than one place, to remind the customer of a tie-in need—extension cords with Christmas trees, or batteries—a prime example. They are needed when a customer buys toys, home-improvement tools, kitchen equipment, cameras, etc. Where will you put your main assortment of batteries? And where will you put an appropriate sampling, to "go with" another purchase? That's cross-merchandising.

If you simply don't have the space to put merchandise in more than one area, use *cross-merchandising signing*. Tell the customer in toys that "Batteries are available in the camera department." Whenever you are signing all those cordless tools that take batteries,

> ## Don't forget your ...
> # BATTERIES!
> ## You'll find AAA to D sizes
> ### Alkaline batteries in Cameras

instead of saying "Batteries not included" say "Batteries available in our camera department." It turns a negative into a service!

Good retailers have made an art of cross-merchandising. When it's strawberry season, the strawberries are presented *with* prepared shortcake or shortcake mix. Pre-sliced vegetables are presented *with* vegetable dips . . . and salad dressings. Is it a service or is it creating impulse purchases? Regardless, it works!

Seriously, there is customer service inherent in this merchandising method. In order to do it successfully, you need to *think like a customer*. And then sign it to tell the customer what you are doing!

For instance, when you are displaying outdoor barbecues,

where is your charcoal starter? Nearby, or in some faraway department? Where are your accessories? Nearby, or in housewares? Where is your charcoal? Nearby, or in your lawn and garden "seasonal" area? Where are your heavy-duty potholders? Where is your grill cleaner? Where are your aprons? Think about it. If you really respect your customers' time, you will make every effort to cross-merchandise. If you can't bring everything together, at least tell them, via signs, where to find what they will want.

To become a better cross-merchandiser, ask yourself these questions:

- 1. What is the main, "destination" product here?

- 2. After I buy that product, what do I need to make it work? Does it need batteries? An electric cord? Accessories?

- 3. What will I need to "finish the project"?

- 4. Does it have "hidden" accessories? If a barbecue needs starter and charcoal, what does this product need in order to get the job done?

- 5. What will I need to clean it up?

- 6. What will I need to store it?

- 7. What can be added to make the product more useful?

All of those questions are helpful in order to develop the most potent sign copy for the products, too. When you have the answers you will have the most persuasive feature benefits.

Think like a customer.

Don't Underestimate Dump Bins

In our chapter on research you'll find how successful dump bins can be. If you use dump bins as a resource for cross-merchandising, your sales results will go from impressive to sensational.

If you sell artificial Christmas trees, for instance, a dump bin of extension cords by the tree display will dramatically accelerate sales—and your reputation for thoughtfulness.

Dump bins have a bad reputation. If overdone, they can look messy. If done badly—with too many items in one dump bin—there can be a swift downgrading of a quality image. But well-planned, well-kept dump bins are little mines of gold—when they are properly placed, disciplined and signed.

Look for High Traffic Bulk Displays

Run a test for yourself, to get an understanding of the impact of this basic. Take an ordinary bulky product that languishes on the bottom of a gondola in your back corner department. Stack it on a main traffic aisle and sign it. Check your sales. Imagine what could be done with a seasonal product?

Bulk displays can be created by putting a sample square of carpet or indoor grass on the floor and stacking product with a sign. It can be done very quickly. Think about this technique to respond to weather-induced needs such as a rack of snow shovels or case stacks of antifreeze.

Summary

Yes, talking about gondola runs, cross-aisle merchandising, endcaps, dump bins and bulk displays is pretty basic stuff. But perhaps it is so basic you just aren't giving each basic enough attention? Think about it. And consider what a good sign can do for each one. ◆

Suggested planogram grid for your
future planning purposes. Use copies
of one section for endcap planning.
Remember: shelves are adjustable.

4. How to Write Effective Sign Copy

ACCORDING TO RESEARCHERS who have gone to the trouble of observing exact eye movements of shoppers as they stroll a store, a sign has a bare microsecond to catch the attention of any potential customer. Thus, brevity *is* wisdom. But being *too* brief can reduce the sign to ineffectiveness. Good sign-writing takes a combination of common sense and sound judgment. Case in point: one sign marked "Apples," and another marked "Granny Smith" or "Jonathan." People do shop for specific apples—they will scan signs for their favorites. "Apples" is not enough. In fact, it is redundant, because it is on a sign hanging over or near an easily recognizable product.

Rule #1: Be Specific Rather Than General

Let's assume you have a hardware store and some nails to sell. An inexperienced signmaker might make the following sign, based on your instructions. It does answer two questions: "What do you have for sale, and what's the price?"

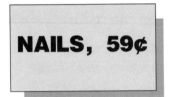

NAILS, 59¢

Problem: the name of the product is too general—it does not answer such typical consumer questions as: "What use are they?" or even more important, "What benefit is this nail to my work?" It hardly answers the most important consumer question, which is, "How much do they cost?" Are they priced by pound or individually? And what customer can decide if nails—by the pound—are a good buy or not? In fact, if they are sold by the pound, how can you even imagine what the bill will be? Customers don't like surprises. Make the pricing as specific as is logical. A suggested improvement would be something like this:

Roofing Nails
Rustproof
25 for 59¢

Rule #2: Make the Pricing Easy to Understand

Customers have become extremely value conscious and they want to be recognized as smart shoppers. Finding a "good buy" is personally satisfying...*so* satisfying that bragging about good buys has become an important part of our social life. People today want to talk about their bargain hunting. Not too long ago, no one—*no one*—talked about the price of anything. It was not polite to discuss money. Now the *value* of a new purchase or service—its *price* is an important part of any conversation.

If you price vegetables by the pound, the average shopper may, while he or she is behind the shopping cart, think he or she is getting a good deal. But at the checkout when they see what they actually paid for a head of lettuce versus what the sign "implied"—they can feel cheated. More and more supermarkets are pricing by individual piece, or by the amount usually purchased. Green peppers, 2 for 75¢, for instance.

If you want your store to be known as an easy, honest and reassuring place to shop—if you want your store to be considered a store for honest values—make your pricing easy to understand.

Every item in your store should have some sort of pricing on it or near enough to it, so the shopper can easily understand the value. Hiding the price simply makes it more difficult to make a sale (unless you are in the fur business, of course).

Rule #3:
Look for Appropriate
"Romance."
Sell the Sizzle

If you have ever read the fine print on a typical restaurant menu, you understand what inappropriate "romance" means. Every noun has three adjectives, everything is always "fresh" and "perfectly seasoned"—until you get your meal. A sign has to communicate in a microsecond, so the romance better be meaningful. Here's an excellent example.

I saw this sign in a fish specialty store in northern Minnesota—where the simple "Fresh salmon" would be a normal sign to expect. However, that "raised in Minnesota" made them sound even more fresh—even more tempting to try. We had salmon for dinner that night. That extra bit of "appropriate romance" was a wonderful selling benefit. "Selling the sizzle" requires creativity. It's not being creative with words—making outrageous puns, for instance. Rather, it is creative listening. Ask your employees why they would buy this particular item; ask your kids; ask your customers. Ask the buyer: is there a unique story about the company, its boss, this product? Every product has a story. Tell it and sell it!

FRESH SALMON

Raised in MINNESOTA

1,000 miles closer to YOU!

$7.99 pound

This sign, in a Minnesota specialty food store, made the salmon sound *days* fresher. Here is how a fact can support a claim of freshness.

Rule #4:
Write Facts, Not Fiction

We are a country suffering from advertising overload. Words like "amazing" and "new improved" have lost their luster. They are overworked. In fact, almost any positive-sounding adjective has been overworked to the point of being unbelievable. They have become fiction.

So look for the facts. Facts such as "raised in Minnesota" when you are dealing with a strong tourist trade—and Minnesotans. Find a fact to support your claim: for freshness, for whatever. The facts have to support or imply benefits, of course.

You may have to work like a private detective to get the facts—but they are worthwhile. Whenever you are tempted to make a claim for "fresh" or somehow "better" ask WHY. WHY is this produce fresher? WHY does it have better flavor? When you get a BECAUSE answer, you get a fact that can be extremely potent on a sign.

New Improved
La-Z-Boy Recliner
Takes just 3" back space
$479 95

A "new improved" recliner might be anything—including a design or upholstery covering. The top sign makes sense to a recliner shopper. It says that the new chair doesn't take so much back space to "recline." It's a real improvement.

New Improved
La-Z-Boy Recliner
$479 95

Rule #5:
Explain What Isn't Obvious

If you have a new product or a new benefit that isn't quickly apparent, you need a sign to tell the customer what's new. A good example is "touchbase" lamps. When they were introduced they looked just like ordinary lamps. They did not have a switch to turn on and off—one simply touched the lamp base. This is not an obvious benefit. This is also not immediately believable. The fastest way to sell these lamps is to have one plugged into an electrical outlet and turned on. Then, via the sign, invite the customer to touch the base and see how easy it is to turn on and off. In this case, a sign just wasn't enough—not for the introduction, anyway. Nothing beats demonstration.

SNAP-OPEN UMBRELLAS

Just push the button on the handle

$12 <u>95</u>

How does it work?

Does the men's jacket have a rain hood hidden in the collar? If it's hidden, the customer won't see it, right? So put "rain hood hidden in collar" on the sign.

Does the umbrella open automatically versus fumbling and pushing it open? Then get "opens automatically" on the

sign. Is the umbrella extra large? "Extra large" and/or "Big enough for 2 people" should appear on the sign. An umbrella is one of those awkward things that people don't want to demonstrate in the store. Help them make a decision without opening it.

Do your paintbrushes have a special bristle that works best when you're using varnish? Tell the customer.

How well does it work?

One-coat Paintbrushes

- **Deluxe paintholding ability**
- **Extra smooth application**

$3⁴⁹

RAINCOATS

● Zip-out winter lining

● Washable shell

99.95

What is hidden to the casual shopper?

Ask yourself these questions, looking for the "gold" mine in any product:

How does it work?

How well does it work?

What is hidden to the casual shopper?

What facts will overcome resistance to a new product? What facts will support a desired claim of extra value? What are its possible new uses?

Buffalo Burgers

- Lower in fat and Lower in cholesterol than beef
- Excellent flavor

$1.89/lb

Pre-shaped Hamburgers

- Perfect bun size
- Easy storage
- Fast defrost and microwave

6 for 2^{19}

Hawaiian Pineapples

$3.49

Flown direct to us!

Sometimes simple facts can make a
product much more appealing.

Rule #6:
Help the Customer
Buy the Best Product

When you are selling functional products, help the customer decide which ones will do the best job. For instance, if you are offering a selection of paint-brushes, organize them by use and sign them by use.

ALL-PURPOSE BRUSHES

For maintenance painting where you don't need a quality

PRO BRUSHES

For latex and oil
Long wearing

SPECIALTY BRUSHES

Trim   Edging
Sash   Special sizes

**Rule #7:
Help the Customer
Comparison Shop Your
Assortment**

If there is any way you can help the customer make a smarter buying decision, or make a decision *faster*, do it. Remember the old Sears catalogs, which always had products presented in a "good, better, best" range? There has never been any better way invented since, to illustrate comparable benefits. You start with the benefits of your basic product; you *add* value to the "better" product by listing why it's better, and *add more value* to the "best" or "deluxe" model. This demands a consistent format, where benefits can be listed in order, so a comparison can be made.

Here is an example. Imagine that you are in a housewares department, and there are four automatic coffeemakers on the shelf. They are arranged from the lowest-price

10-CUP
COFFEEMAKER

-Lighted on/off switch

$29.95

10-CUP
COFFEEMAKER

- Lighted on/off switch
- Automatic drip-stop
- Cord storage

$31.95

HOW TO WRITE EFFECTIVE SIGN COPY

to the highest. There are four signs, one for each product.

Notice that the benefits are listed in similar order on each sign, so the additional benefits are easy to see and one can quickly decide which benefit is worth the extra money. Such an arrangement becomes a silent selling tool and is considered "customer service" by the consumer. It also helps "trade up" the customer.

This arrangement can work in a grocer's deli case, in a display of camping equipment, with do-it-yourself tools, with baby cribs and strollers—any situation where you have a selection of merchandise in one category. Such signing will be appreciated by the customer and is almost permanent signing—hence low-maintenance—for you.

10-CUP COFFEEMAKER

- Lighted on/off switch
- Automatic shut-off
- Programmable start

$34.95

10-CUP COFFEEMAKER

- Lighted on/off switch
- Automatic shut-off
- Program start and brewtime
- 23-K gold-plated filter

$38.95

Rule #8:
Remind the Customer
of Logical Needs:
Cross Merchandise

An important part of customer service is also self-serving: it is suggestion selling. When a customer is in your paint department, you should have a sign with a checklist.

This type of signing is common in most paint departments today. There are opportunities elsewhere. Every good shoe salesperson will ask every customer who buys shoes, "How about polish/cleaner/preservative for those shoes?" When your shoe department becomes self-service, you need that sign suggesting these products. How many of you have bought a toy and forgotten that it takes batteries before it works? There are enormous amounts of merchandise that take batteries,

DO YOU NEED?

Paintbrush cleaner

Brushes

Trays

Rollers

Roller extender

Trim sets

Patching plaster

from hand-held kitchen tools to cameras. Where is your helpful suggestion-selling sign? (This subject is discussed in Chapter 2 but is well worth repeating. There are just too many opportunities missed.)

Rule #9:
Always Ask, What
Will it Save?

Help clinch the sale. Many times the customer wants the product, but may feel a little bit guilty about buying it. He or she needs a rationale—or a rationalization. Aside from the lure of a big price cut, what can you offer? Consider what is valuable to the customer and find out if the product offers any assistance:

Will it save money? 50% off is magic. But you can't afford large markdowns every day. Think in terms of dollars whenever possible. "Save $10 today" might be 10 or 20% off—but it sounds like more and is instantly recognizable. Percentages always have to be mentally translated by the customer. That takes time. He or she doesn't have time. This one tip could save you hundreds, maybe thousands of dollars by itself. Before you automatically take a large percentage off, see if a dollar amount will have the same effect. Test both ways, via signing. (See the chapter on Testing.)

GE Cordless Hand Mixer
For fast, light duty

Takes 4 "A" batteries
from our Camera Dept.

$17.99

Will it save time? People today are extremely busy and pressed for time. Often they will spend *more* money to save *time.* Will this product cut work time in half? Make clean-up easier? Faster? Saving time is a key benefit that should be spelled out on your sign.

If you deliver, gift wrap, consolidate packages at a service desk, or pick up returns—anything you do that saves customers time and aggravation—put it on the merchandise selling sign!

Paintliners

Disposable
Easy cleanup

3 for 39¢

Recliner

SALE

Buy it today

We'll deliver it next week

Paintliners are the answer to the messy problem of painting cleanup. Without a sign, who knows what, or where, they are?

Add your service message whenever it makes buying more convenient to the customer.

Will it save the planet? People are interested in conserving energy, conserving wildlife, conserving quality water resources. If the product has been revised to be ecologically sound, tell the customer. It could tip the scales and make another sale.

Recycling is becoming a standard in our society. Show people your concern.

GLASS PLUS

- Shines glass without streaks
- No phosphates
--Recyclable, refillable container

$3.49

WE RECYCLE all boxes

IF YOU CHANGE YOUR CAR'S OIL,

drop off the dirty oil here.

We'll take care of it SAFELY.

Will it save me stress? Is it easier to handle? Does it make cooking, fixing up or cleaning easier? Are instructions easy to understand? Is it simpler to use? Consider, with the graying of America, how many older people have arthritis and difficulty with buttons, laces, medicine caps—especially "childproof" ones, and such "improvements" as twist-off bottle caps. That's why pull-on pants and tops are attractive to older people. That's why shoes with velcro fasteners make sense over laces. They have hidden benefits that need to be offered in a sign.

Rule #10:
Don't Say the Obvious

There are certain words and phrases that make their way into retail lingo that should be stricken from the language. One is "assorted colors." The customer can see the colors right there on the shelf or rack. Edit such phrases out. If there's nothing left to say you don't need a sign.

Walking Shoes

- Velcro "laces"
- Easy to slip on and
- Easy to slip off
- No untied laces problem

$34 ⁹⁵

Rule #11:
Break All the Rules
If It Fits Your Strategy

If you decide that you are an old-fashioned hardware store, selling nails from kegs, or by the pound, then do it. But do it consistently. If you are a specialty old-time candy store, sign the way old-time stores did. If your store has a marvelous sense of humor, use humor. Break a few price rules.

Hot Dogs 75¢
2 for $1.75

Our
COFFEE
is so RICH it votes
REPUBLICAN

Any husband ordering
CUSTOM-BLENDED
PAINT
must have his
wife's
written permission

Rule #12:
Stay Positive, Sign Friendly

Try not to give your customers a list of "don'ts" or commandments. You are supposed to be welcoming people into your store, not improving their manners (even though manners could stand improvement!). Look at the difference between these signs for the same thing.

☞ **NO SHIRT,**

☞ **NO SHOES,**

☞ **NO SERVICE!**

SHIRT AND SHOES

ARE REQUIRED

BY STATE LAW.

THANK YOU

THANK YOU

FOR

NOT SMOKING

NO SMOKING

EMPLOYEES ONLY

NO ADMITTANCE

NO CREDIT CARDS

IN ORDER TO KEEP PRICES LOW, WE DO NOT ACCEPT CREDIT CARDS

Ask about our Express Check-Cashing Service

Rule #13:
Listen to the People Who Answer Customers' Questions

If your signing isn't right, people will ask questions. Who answers them? That person is key to getting your signing right. Of course, not everything can be answered via signs. But a great deal of the obvious can. And that's why you need consistent feedback from the field, from the firing line, as to what is motivating customers and what troubles them. A good writer is a superb listener. A good writer listens to customers complain, to customers who return merchandise, and to customers who praise a product. "Oh, what do you like best about it?" That's where you will

"I HEARD CUSTOMERS ASK ABOUT..."

Please tell us what you heard...on these cards. Thanks for your help!

find a gold mine of information and motivating copy. If you had a system which allowed the people who deal with the customers to write the signs, (with good direction) you would have the best possible system.

There are several ways to trigger employee feedback. One is a store tour with lots of questions—writing down the answers from employees. Another help: put up a sign at the employee "punchout" spot that asks for help. ◆

5. Pricing Strategies and the Signs They Need

THERE ARE FOUR BASIC PRICING PHILOSOPHIES: promotional, everyday low, competitor-reactive and high-service (usually high tech). In real life, many retailers have created hybrid mixes of one or two of the four basics. In order to be really well understood by the customer, however, one philosophy should be dominant in your store.

Signing for Promotional Pricing

Promotional pricing means that your store depends upon advertising and that ad sales are a significant part of your day-to-day business. The primary function of your signing is to *support your advertising.*

If there is one cardinal rule for advertising, it is this: sign every advertised item. If the item is important enough to be advertised, it is important enough to sign. It is your duty to the customer to help that person find your advertised merchandise. It is your duty to make shopping easier and faster.

How do you guarantee signing consistency? By tying your buyer's or manager's request for advertising to a sign request. Or, by having your advertising writers write the sign copy.

If your organization is large enough to have a separate signing department, simply have your ad request form made in triplicate—one copy goes to the advertising person, one copy goes to the sign department,

> *If there is one cardinal rule for advertising, it is this: sign every advertised item.*

and one copy is kept by the buyer. Any changes in price, assortment, or item, demands another triplicate request. That way, you keep last-minute changes going to the sign shop as well as the ad department. This is a typical methodology for large companies.

There is a second way, utilizing a separate sign department, which helps give greater consistency to the ad and sign message. Your sign department uses corrected advertising copy proofs as the source for all signs. Thus, the headline or major copy point in the ad gets on the sign. This process also works well when you have a small organization and depart

ment managers may be making the signs.

That process takes care of the production of the signs. Now, you need precise responsibilities for signing *in the store* to make sure each and every sign is up when it is supposed to be up, and taken down immediately after the event or promotion is over. You can make each department head responsible for each department—but that dilutes responsibility. The ideal is to have one person in the store who has total responsibility for signing. That person tours the store with the advertisement in hand, checking that every item has a sign. That person keeps touring the store, to make sure that, if you should run out of ad merchandise, you set up your raincheck or ad merchandise substitution system—and its signing.

This person is also responsible for taking down signs after a sale event is over—taking down seasonal signs that are out of date—making sure that there are no references to St. Patrick's Day on March 18—making sure that you are never embarrassed by an out-of-date sign.

This person does need some

general guidelines from management. For instance, when does spring start in your store? Are you fashion forward, or behind the official calendar date? When does "spring" end in your store, and summer references start? When will you officially begin "fall" and that all important holiday season? Some stores won't allow Christmas merchandise on their floors before Halloween—others send their Christmas catalogs out in October! What are your rules? Don't take these "generalities" for granted. When your motives or desires are unclear, people will assume —and do—the worst! It is much better for one of your trusted employees to be inspecting your signs—than having your customers think you are making mistakes, are sloppy—or misleading with your signs!

A second cardinal rule: sign beyond your advertising. If you are advertising a name-brand

---

The second cardinal rule: sign beyond your advertising.

---

product at a market-low price, of course you will give it a sale sign. But you can sign other, non-sale merchandise on the shelf, too. Their prices get a "halo" effect from your price-setting advertising. You may have customers trading themselves up to another product in your line—at better profits for you.

If you carry private label product, be sure you sign and price it competitively with your brands so that you can convert some of the customers responding to your brand-driving advertising to your higher-margin private labels.

Whenever you are planning a price promotion, analyze your clearances and check the dates

on old merchandise. High traffic periods are the best way to get rid of clearances. Make sure they are properly priced: recently marked down, or marked down even further just before the sale. Then dramatize the clearance with a sign that clearly spells out the savings. Nothing beats 50% off!

Advertising is an invitation—an invitation to visit your store. So make sure that your store is inviting. Check that your semi-permanent signs aren't dog-eared, that displays are well stocked and tidy, that advertised items are clearly positioned and signed. Make sure you have maximized the "halo" effect on allied merchandise—that you have your private-labeled product priced and signed. Double-check your clearance areas. Then unlock the doors!

Signing for EDL Pricing

The everyday-low-price store advertises to the customer that its daily prices are satisfactorily low—no need to wait for a sale. Prices are usually somewhere between normal markup and a strong sale price. Competitive shopping is aggressive to maintain the EDL image.

The mainstream signing for everyday low is simple and could be delegated to department level. Once the overall message is decided and impressed via pre-printing on all your signs, the selection of items, their features and prices is relatively easy. Since prices don't change as often as they do in a promotional series of sales, signs can remain up for indefinite periods.

There are a few warnings about controlling EDL: first, since signing will positively affect sales, the selection of merchandise to be signed should be controlled so that sufficient stock is available to support increased sales. Some guidance is necessary to help departments select timely items to sign and to control how many items will be signed.

Everyday-low prices can be advertised, so some method of supporting all advertising needs to be in place. Some method needs to be created to identify any price-off merchandise as separate from everyday low—both inside the company and in signing for the customer. This can be done by having more than one pre-printed format of sign card stock available for the sign-maker.

The idea of toppers and other enhancements can be vastly simplified in the EDL strategy, substituting the promotional store's calendar of sale events with a few specific sign programs that can stay in place for months—even all year !

#1: Baseline EDL signing

General merchandise signing should be substantial in an everyday-low pricing strategy, if for no other reason than to convince the customer that prices are, indeed, low.

There are ways to suggest low price, yet everyday price. The following examples could be used as pre-printed "toppers" for your everyday price items:

- VALUE PRICED
- CHECK OUR LOW PRICE
- EVERYDAY SPECIAL VALUE
- OUR DISCOUNT PRICE
- EVERY DAY LOW PRICE
- ANOTHER GREAT BUY

#2: Temporary promotions in an EDL environment

There are times when EDL stores will want to promote. A manufacturer has given them a deal and they wisely want to pass on the savings. There was a price break on a category of merchandise. For competitive reasons they want to put a product on sale. For whatever reason, the item is undergoing a *temporary* price change for the customer. There can be many reasons why a price can change. Your decision is whether to have a separate program for each reason, or give all price breaks an overall name or "generic" sign topper that fits into an EDL environment. Here are some samples of names for these promotions:

- T.L.P.—Temporarily Lowered Price
- Special Purchase/Special Price
- Manufacturer's Special
- Extra Value, Extra Savings
- Unadvertised Special
- Customer Appreciation Special
- Advertised Special
- Sale

#3: Special value programs

Look in your stock for merchandise that fits this criteria: seasonal, highly desirable but relatively basic. If you were to select one item from this stock and take a lower markup on it *for the entire season,* how much more could you sell? Probably quite a lot, if you were to sign and promote it as a special value program in your department.

Here are some sample headings for this part of the EDL strategy:

- SUPER VALUE
- VERY SPECIAL BUY
- VSP: VERY SPECIAL PRICE
- OUR BEST BUY
- DISCOUNT SPECIAL
- GUARANTEED VALUE
- VALUE PRICED

You may want to consider doing this on a weekly or monthly basis—not for the entire season. Be sure you indicate the time factor, to help give urgency to your message:

SUPER VALUE of the WEEK
SUPER VALUE of the MONTH
OUR SEPTEMBER SPECIAL
PRE-CHRISTMAS PRICE

> *Everyday low prices need everyday confirmation, via signing, that they are low.*

#4: Permanently lowered prices

As a product goes from its peak selling period into a time when it is frequently promoted (by promotional-price competition), the EDL store may opt to permanently lower the price of its merchandise to some point between the promotional store's new and sale price.

There may be a general price break on the merchandise everywhere. Or, you simply see declining sales but don't want to go on clearance. Here is a big opportunity for EDL strategies to support their claims of low prices. Signing such opportunities could include:

- NEW LOW PRICE
- WE CUT OUR PRICES AGAIN!
- ROLLED BACK PRICE
- PRICE BREAK !

Everyday low prices need everyday confirmation, via signing, that they are low. A sign indicates that you are proud of your price and implies a special price to your customer. Without sales to excite customers, the EDL merchant must *look* promotional and exciting—hence, a heavy use of signing. And the heavy use of euphemisms for the word "sale."

A well-thought-out selection of programs from the above lists could make EDL signing rather simple to implement, with a maximum effect on the customer's image of the store.

Signing for a Reactive Competitive-Price Strategy

This strategy is commonly used by the small independent against the giants. This strategy depends upon heavy advertising by competition. You, as the smaller independent, simply take competition's ads or prices and use them in signs to indicate your lower prices.

You need to be able to change prices on a dime, and make sure that your price changes are disciplined. Ideally, you would have automatic price changing abilities with scanning. If you don't, careful price-break signs need to be made for all your checkouts.

A simple sign format can be used, since you are using competition's ad copy for your features/benefits:

Take competition's ads and use them in signs to indicate your lower prices.

The reactive-strategy users have several possible claims to support their pricing. One is "We comparison shop for you." The basic claim is that, with a shopping basket of the same merchandise purchased at Store A and at Store B, a customer would save money shopping at Store B. This competition-based strategy demands a cadre of comparison shoppers and the ability to change prices

regularly. Disciplined records need to be kept to support your claim—and it is one that the Better Business Bureaus will probably investigate.

Another stance is the offer to match any bona fide price from any competitor, whether it be sale or regular shelf price. This strategy really doesn't set you apart from competition today, but it does achieve parity. One word of warning: if you don't want to bite the bullet and honestly meet every competitors' price, don't do it. You can develop a litany of exceptions to meeting competition. Search through your competition carefully and make sure you are going to be able to execute exactly what you claim. If a store has a one-day sale, or a 13-hour sale, will you honor its advertised prices precisely during those time periods and no more? That's fair, but be sure it

Check OUR Prices!

JONES'
Widgets
000⁰⁰

Our Low Price:
00⁰⁰

We're LOWER Again

JONES'
Deluxe
Widgets
000⁰⁰

OUR Price:
00⁰⁰

is clear to the customer. If a competitor has a close-out with limited quantities, what will you do with your substantial quantities? If a competitor offers something "free" with purchase, how will you react? On this page and the next are four sample signs supporting this strategy.

WE GUARANTEE LOW PRICES

If you find a lower price anywhere, we will match it...

...if it is first quality merchandise

...if it is identical to our stock

WE TRY TO HAVE THE LOWEST PRICES IN TOWN. IF YOU FIND A LOWER PRICE, LET US KNOW.

If it's identical merchandise and first quality like ours, we'll match the price for you and thank you!

REWARD!

If you find a lower regular price in town, let us know. We'll give you a $5.00 merchandise credit!

WE WANT TO HAVE THE LOWEST PRICES EVERY DAY!

WE WILL MATCH ANY AND ALL ADVERTISED SALE PRICES!

Just bring in any competitor's ad, and if we have the merchandise, you get the advertised price.

THANK YOU!

Above: note the term "in town" which sounds friendly, but also gives a territorial limit to your policy.

Signing for a High-service Strategy

High service is usually associated with a higher price. The product is either large—like furniture; complicated—like electronics, or very valuable—like jewelry. All these products can be daunting to a customer. Retailers have the challenge of having an adequate amount of salespeople available for customers who may take considerable time to decide on a purchase. Salespeople need to have excellent technical knowledge of the product. Even so, people will be shy about asking for help. Thus, the signing can be an "introductory kit" to the salesperson.

High service means more than having capable salespeople. The people on the sales floor need support signing. They need policy signs that clearly spell out your important

IF YOU'RE INTERESTED
IN A MULTI-ROOM SOUND SYSTEM

Brand Name	Component	Price
Magnavox ST-44	Receiver	$000.00
	Speakers	00.00
Panasonic System	Receiver	000.00
	Tape Deck	00.00
	Speakers	00.00
Bose RX	Speakers	00.00

IF YOU DEMAND
THE ABSOLUTE BEST SOUND

Brand Name	Component	Price
Magnavox ST-44	Receiver	$000.00
	Speakers	00.00
Panasonic System	Receiver	000.00
	Tape Deck	00.00
	Speakers	00.00
Bose RX	Speakers	00.00

Sign for customer service by relating your branded products to the customer's needs. These signs group products into three general areas for sound systems: multi-room, top of the line, and (next page) space limitations.

IF SPACE IS LIMITED

Brand Name	Component	Price
Sony Max	Receiver	$000.00
	Turntable	000.00
Yamaha 2000	CD Player	000.00
	Tape Deck	000.00
	Speakers	000.00
Soundesign	Receiver	000.00
	Turntable	000.00

guarantees, return policy, delivery system, etc. It is their "back-up" when a customer gets too demanding or cranky. It is something for customers to study while they are browsing. High-service retailers who have switched their signing from handwritten to printed signs have discovered that the customer respects the printed signs. With handwritten copy the customer was more likely to demand price negotiations—they didn't believe it was a firm price. With printed signs, the price is recognized as firm. Any negotiating below it would be a pleasant surprise!

High service demands larger, 11 x 14″ signs to help customers make decisions. This sort of signing is usually seen in electronics and physical fitness departments where customers are really unsure about what is best for their needs. Signs can be as straight-forward as "How to Select the Right Bicycle," or "What to Look for in 35mm Cameras." You are translating manufacturers' information, condensing it into a mini-poster. A sign is taking the place of a trained salesperson.

You might, with permission, quote *Consumer Reports* magazine and give the rankings of the products you carry. You might create your own rankings, based on customers' priorities.

High service strategies usually have more counter displays with manufacturers' handouts available. The emphasis is on giving information.

We've discussed cross-selling in other chapters—it works well here.

PATIO FURNITURE

Table	$89.95
Chairs, each	29.95
Umbrella	79.95
6-Pc. Set	$279.00

It's smart to use a larger sign and price each piece, then give a total price for a typically-purchased grouping. Ideally if you offered terms, you would indicate on the sign what a 6-month contract would cost per month. Do as much math as possible for the customer!

We've discussed checklist signing in other chapters—it applies here.

When you are showing a room setting or patio setting, there is an option for another sign called "combination signing." Let's say you sign each piece of the patio set with features/benefits and price. What is the price for the whole set? With and without umbrella? Create a combination sign that adds it all up for the customer. And if you have terms, what it would cost per month.

If you have a room setting, of course you price each piece. But what if the customer likes the entire room and it fits her home perfectly? Not an unusual occurrence. Encourage the thought. Create a combination sign listing the pieces and giving a total. This is most successful with children's furniture and knock-down furniture arrangements which are in the lower price ranges—but I have seen enough people buy "the whole room" so I have faith in the strategy no matter what the total price.

> *The first rule about hybrids: keep one strategy dominant.*

Hybrids: How to Combine Strategies

Your store may opt to be promotionally priced, yet want a reputation for low everyday pricing, too. In that case, some part of the EDL strategy might be adapted. An EDL store might want more traffic and opt for more promotions on a short-term basis: advertise and add the sale signing. Just be very sure that you don't confuse the customer. If you are planning any major change, test it first on a focus group or advisory group of your customers. Test it on a group of non-customers to see if it will motivate them. Store executives can agonize over a campaign for months and forget to ask the most important person—their customer. Make sure that the customers' confidence won't be shaken by your planned change in strategy. Make sure that you have an understandable strategy. Make sure you aren't over promising. Listen to what the customers say about your new slogan. Have them put it into their words. And perhaps their words will be better than your copywriter's! Then execute.

The first rule about hybrids: keep one strategy dominant. Don't try to do a little bit of everything in the store—you'll stand for nothing.

Another rule: use color to "label" and clarify your programs. Make sure that each program has a distinct color and distinct copy differences.

Third rule: make sure your programs are well understood by all your employees. Communicate the differences. Test the differences. Give your store people badges that say, "Ask me about" and name your strategy. They'll be forced to know the program you're pushing. ◆

6. How to Test Prices and Items via Signs

PRICING CAN BE AN ART. A wonderful example is a direct-mail expert from southern Minnesota who made bird-baths and tried to sell them via small-space ads in the back of shelter magazines. His original casting cost was very low. He priced his first birdbaths at $9.99. No sales. Did he go down in price? No, he *raised* his price in the next series of ads—to $14.99. When he got to $18.99 he found the magic price point. Then people perceived value and thought that the birdbath was "worthwhile"—that it was going to last a few seasons. (The fact that the shelter magazines cater to middle and above incomes may have had something to do with it.) The point: you don't always have to *lower* the price to make it right.

How to Set "Magic" Price Points

There are magic numbers. These are numbers that are price hurdles to people. They are willing to pay "up to $5" for some things, and "up to $10" for others, and so forth up through $100. If you can price your product just *under* those magic numbers, you can increase sales. And you can frequently *increase* your prices (yet stay under the magic number) and improve your margins. Does the customer really balk at spending $4.89 versus $4.69? Or $9.99 instead of $8.59? It's worth a test.

One-store price tests take time since you have to present the merchandise for a week or two at one price, and then the same length of time at a different price. Your test is simply how much you sold at each price. Everything else should remain equal: assortment, space, location, signing, length of time.

There are magic numbers

Always price lower the first week, then go up. Don't penalize customers who bought first and might resent the price going down one week later.

Two-store tests are faster, but do add that fudge factor of having two stores with different locations and possibly different customer demographics—as well as store disciplines. You must have confidence in each store's capacity to stay in stock, etc. But you do know, at the end of a week or two, whether you can sell the same amount at $4.89 as you do at $4.69. Just be sure the stores are staying in full assortment, with consistent space, location and signing.

How to Test for Increased Sales via Multiple Pricing

A gray area that doesn't get its due is the testing of multiple prices. Certain products such as underwear and socks are usually purchased in multiples. Are you signing to encourage it? Other products may not normally be purchased in multiples, but customers may buy two or three (versus one) if encouraged to do so. Pricing such products in multiples can really pay off in extra sales. They definitely should be tested and signing is the way to do it. Even something with a price over $15 or $20, such as men's summer pants, should be tested, if the multiple is under a "magic number" like $40 or $50. It's worth a try. Using a sign is the easiest way and the cheapest to get a reading on customer acceptance. Sign one store with a single price, sign a second

Men's twill pants

Washable

$24.00

Men's twill pants

Washable

2 for $48.00

$24.00 each

Sign one store with a single price, sign a second store with a multiple price. (Be sure the single price is in the second sign, but not the feature.)

store with a multiple price. (Be sure the single price is in the second sign, but not the feature.)

Once you have an indication of the general sales impact of multiple pricing, you can project what would happen if you advertised that way. For instance, you know what happens when you advertise $24.00 pants for $19.99. What will happen when you advertise pants for 2 for $39.98? Test it by signing and projecting the difference.

SALE
Summer Pants
benefit, benefit
2 pairs for $39.98
$19.99 each

SALE
Summer pants
benefit, benefit
$19.99

Once you have an indication of the general sales impact of multiple pricing, you can project what would happen if you advertised that way. Test it by signing and projecting the difference.

How to Use Signs to Test New Products

Large chains select test stores which have similar demographics and customer count. These stores have test locations on high-traffic aisles, where merchandise can be presented consistently. Buyers and store executives communicate regularly about the strength or weakness of specific items which have been selected for test. Sales are checked daily and monitored by store. Any deviation causes a phone call to the test store. Did you get the merchandise out? Is it signed? What's not happening? Or, why did you sell so much more than the other stores?

Here's a vivid example of the potential problems of this kind of testing. A small apparel chain put 12 glitter sweaters in each test store. One store sold six the first day. They were ecstatic. They thought they had the trend of the century. When the buyer called the store, however, she discovered that the six were purchased by a soon-to-be-bride for her bridesmaids. Reconsidering, the bride returned them the next day—happily before the 50% sell-through could be acted upon.

Buyers usually are testing trends—getting an idea of the acceptability of some new accessory, color, or style change. A sample group put on the floor and signed this week, with successful sales, can trigger a large reorder and an ad. And the security of having invested in a proven winner.

Whenever You're Testing, a Few Words of Caution

Whenever you are doing something out of the ordinary—such as a test—be sure, absolutely sure, that you have told the store personnel everything about what you are doing. Be sure they understand testing and that you want a real result. You do not want them to participate in some way to increase sales just to increase sales. They should understand that the effort should be consistent with other stores. This isn't a sales contest. It is a survey of customer responses, with equal effort presented by each store.

Now, how to evaluate the results. This is not a formula. This is experience. Once you have established your test stores, you need to watch them and watch their performance under various circumstances. Some stores perform better in "sale" conditions than others. Often this is a surprise. The elite suburb will often generate more off-price sales than a downtown store or a blue-collar store.

Once you have a handle on this, you can project what the tests mean in terms of promoting a product as well as general day-to-day sales. It takes time and a diary and day-to-day monitoring of sales.

The point of all this is:

• A sign and careful monitoring can give you just the information you need to reorder and promote a product.

• A sign and careful monitoring can increase sales by helping you sell more than one item— multiple sales transactions.

• A sign and careful monitoring can help you establish the most acceptable price (at the best profit margin) for any product that isn't under competitive attack.

• A sign can teach you a great deal with a minimum of risk and investment.

That's successful marketing. Every department, no matter how basic the business, should be testing something. And every "test" should have a sign. In fact, every store should have a formalized testing program which has a sign as an integral part of the program. It will successfully speed up consumers' reaction to and acceptance of the new product. Speed is all-important in getting a handle on new trends. ◆

7. Enhancing Your Signs for Special Events or Strategies

White Sales, Electronics Sales, Semi-Annual Clearances, D.A. (Day-After) Sales, 13-Hour Sales, E.O.M. Clearances, Pre-Season Sales, Sunshine Sales, Birthday Sales, Thanksgiving Sales, Crazy Days, Moonlight Madness Sales—what do all these sales have in common? Only one thing: they are repeated year after year; some of them are repeated monthly or seasonally. That makes them candidates for special signing, and possibly the addition of those extra strips of cardboard that sit on top of a sign-holder and are called, rightfully, "toppers." A topper literally goes on top of your merchandise sign. It may be a pre-printed sheet of cardboard or plastic that sticks above your merchandise sign. Or, a topper may be the top of your sign, which is pre-printed, usually in reverse or a color, to indicate a special event or seasonal promotion.

If a sale is big enough, it could be worthy of investment in toppers. If the sale is repeated, it could be worth making the toppers in flexible plastic, so they are easy to store and will stay in good shape for the next go-round of the event. Your stores, of course, need a storage system and encouragement to take good care of the toppers.

Toppers are typically used for store-wide sales—to identify advertised merchandise and also to add color and excitement to the sale. Take care in selecting the type and colors. If you are investing in plastic, you want the style to last several years. So, keep it classic. Don't use black or very dark backgrounds—they may look sharp in layout stage, or when you're looking at one or two. When you have a sea of them in the store, it can look overwhelming and depressing. On the other hand, use high contrast between type and background, for easy reading.

By using toppers, you simplify the copy on the sign itself. No need to repeat "Birthday Sale Special" on every sign— it's on the topper. There is something about toppers that conveys excitement. The customer has been trained—and will gravitate to merchandise with toppers over signs, believing that "This is really special." Use them when you have an event that deserves them.

Toppers don't have to be used exclusively for sales, either. They can be a regular part of your signing program, pointing out weekly or monthly specials, a unique value campaign you are consistently presenting, or even a new trend. Here are some examples:

- NEWS for the 90's

- Another great fashion idea from Smith's

- Another Brand Name Value

- Fall Fashion Festival

- Unadvertised Special for our special customers

- As Advertised

- Value of the Month

- Our Weekly SPECIAL

- Another BRAND NAME Value

If the idea of toppers is just too complicated and expensive for you, there is a simple solution. Have your choice of the above headings pre-printed on your signs. The pre-printing can be done in a bright, contrasting color and will work much as a "topper" without any of its expense. There is another hidden benefit to this simpler program: when the sale or event is over, the sign *has* to come down. With separate toppers, store people may be tempted to remove the topper, but keep the promotional-price sign up after the sale has ended. Such practices are difficult to discipline. With the event printed right on the sign itself, it is easy to take down all the sale signs at once.

To summarize, you can utilize "toppers" (either separately or integrated in your signs) successfully for:

- Store-wide sales events

- Seasonal introductions

- The introduction of new products or trends

- Departmental events

- Ongoing promotional campaigns (Weekly Special, etc.)

- Identifying clearances throughout the store

- Simply identifying whatever has been advertised with an "As Advertised"

- Identifying key gift ideas during pre-holiday gift-giving periods

EVERYDAY LOW PRICE

CLEARANCE

AS ADVERTISED

SALE!

AS ADVERTISED

EVERYDAY LOW PRICE

Enhancements

Simple changes in paper color can create a dramatic change in the total sign presentation in a department—or the store. Consider changing the sign paper from white background to a bright yellow for spring, pale pink or green for holidays, orange for Halloween. (An additional benefit of the orange signs for Halloween is that, come November 1, you can quickly identify and take down all your Halloween signs.)

Look at your overall sign program and select the most appropriate for a color change. Then decide which events or programs would benefit the most by being set apart. Use yellow only for clearances, for instance. Orange for new products or trends. Or only for your weekly or monthly special values. Don't forget the discipline factor. How difficult will it be to maintain your planned program? Who will discipline the program and make sure that the right merchandise gets the special treatment? Plan the program, as well as the signing.

There are other ideas for your signs. Consider stick-on circles or "badges" as a possibility, particularly as an alternative to toppers. They might add the right touch to a "Certified Value," for instance. This is a hand operation which limits the quantities, but can be very attention-getting.

You might want to preprint

> *In most sign programs, the difficulty is not in originating the ideas but in disciplining the implementation.*

all your signing materials with a one-color version of your logo, discreetly at the bottom, top or side-corner of the sign card stock. It is easy to set your signing up to allow for that space. Other messages besides your logo can, of course, be used. It has to be a very short, small message, or your sign copy will lose space—and lose effectiveness.

In most sign programs, the difficulty is not in originating the ideas but in disciplining the implementation. How many toppers can one department handle? When does an important sign message get lost in colors, a pre-printed logo and an attached stick-on badge? If a sign is created which has, for instance, three elements—that is, product information which should include price and customer benefits, *plus* a topper, *plus* your store logo—the chance of the key message getting lost is guaranteed. You have added one too many elements. Use the rule of simplification: one price/benefit sign, one additional element. No more.

It is possible, by working with the right sign-making supplier, to have a unique background designed and supplied at low cost. A do-it-yourself store, for instance, might want a slight wood-grain background:

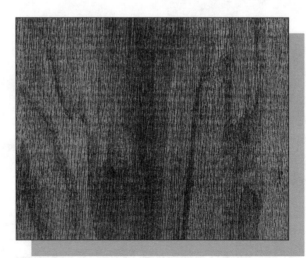

A store with a strong color theme might want a color border around every sign. If you want to reinforce your store slogan or price message, pre-print it on every sign. Such enhancements have a two-fold effect: they add uniqueness to your promotional efforts and they can add spark to your presentations. Customers will respond and so will your associates. Everyone will feel that something special is going on here. Just keep it simple and keep it disciplined!

Once your promotional calendar is set, it is easy to plan exactly what promotional signing will go with each event. Then cost the entire package, and thus establish a promotional sign budget. The calendar and the expected sales from each event should help you set priorities. ◆

A typical worksheet:

	EVENTS CALENDAR		# OF ITEM SIGNS, EST.		SPECIAL SIGN COLOR		TOPPERS		POSTERS		BANNERS		DISPLAYS	
	#	COST	#	COST	#	COST	#	COST	#	COST	#	COST	#	COST
Jan.														
Feb.														
Mar.														
Apr.														
May														
Jun														
Jul														
Aug														
Sep														
Oct														
Nov														
Dec														
TOTAL														

8. One Year of In-Store Promotions

AJOR DEPARTMENT STORES have made the start of each season an in-store art form: the red or green carpet is unrolled, seasonal trims and flower arrangements appear overnight, aisles of banners announce "It's spring" or "It's back-to-school" or "It's Christmas!" On the other hand, you could go into some stores any day of the year and barely discern a difference. Somewhere in between lies a standard for your store.

A very economical way to say "something has changed" and give a fresh look is to use a different background color for all your signing. If that calls for too many sign changes, simply change the background color for signs that highlight new, seasonal merchandise. At the end of the season make sure you replace those signs, change to a new background color, and use it for the next season's new merchandise. You will be emphasizing newness and freshening your in-store look at least four times a year.

There was a specialty store in New York which took display to its limits. It repainted the walls in a bright new color every season—for a small store, not such a difficult task. The act did tell customers that this store believed in change, and in being very up to date. Assuming you can't go to such lengths, what can you do?

Month by Month . . .

January: Sales and Clearances. It's Bargain Month. It's a time when customers make resolutions, diet and start exercise programs. What can you do to tie in with these ideas? Look for a way to colorfully tie all your bargains together into one major signing campaign. "Start the New Year Bright" as well as right. It's a good time for a baby sale, a fitness sale that includes equipment, accessories, diet and health foods and gym apparel. It's also tax preparation time: promote home office supplies, calculators, files, ways to get organized. Look for ways to collect, display and sign merchandise that addresses your customers' immediate needs. Sign for impulse purchases. Sign displays that encourage "add-on" purchases. Sign to show respect for and recognition of Martin Luther King day on January 15.

February: the month for Valentine's Day. Use red for gift sign borders or use pink for gift sign card stock. Paste a heart on your gift-oriented signs. Toppers? Consider using small red ribbons tied to the signholder.

Food operations can get creative—going beyond the heart-shaped candy box to unique gift "baskets": a colander filled with premium spaghetti mixes, spaghetti and white utensils. A cooking pot full of canned soups with a gift tag that says "I'll make lunch every Saturday!" There are hundreds of possibilities.

March: St. Patrick's Day. Turn the ribbons to green.

"Goodbye to Winter" Sale

35% OFF
All Wool Skirts

March 21 is Earth Day—a new event that may remind you of the 1960's, but is mainstream today. Look for opportunities to tie in to Earth Day. Promote your biodegradable, ecosystem-friendly merchandise and sign accordingly. Put your garbage bags on special and sponsor a neighborhood cleanup effort with local boy scouts, Golden K's, or other active group. Look for local groups who support recycling, and look for ways you can tie into their efforts and increase traffic. Never forget to sign what you're doing. Always tell the customer any good news. Look for a spot at your checkout as a permanent location for good "institutional" signing.

March/April: Easter. Lavender or yellow ribbons? Consider signing all new spring apparel with yellow-colored card stock. Toppers of artwork or photographs of fresh, colorful spring flowers say "fresh" and "new" without a word of copy.

A specialty store in New York took display to its limits. It repainted the walls in a bright new color every season.

April: everybody's gardening. Take advantage of the greening. Bring back your St. Patrick's Day green ribbons. When is your official, in-store day when spring starts? Declare a "spring cleaning" day for your store and make sure it is looking especially bright and tidy. Clean stockrooms, too.

A late Wednesday in April is Secretary's Day!

May: Mother's Day. Not a lavender-themed event anymore. Mothers are young, fashion-aware and apt to get a house-repair kit as well as lingerie. Break out of traditional thinking and think of unusual Mother's Day gift ideas. (Please, not a vacuum cleaner!) Again, tie ribbons on the display product or signholders. Or use signs with built-in toppers. Use signs to announce the *date* of Mother's Day—it's different every year and confusing to customers. A reminder of the date creates urgency.

May 5 is Mexican Revolution Day which is a big fiesta event that is celebrated in many places, especially the American Southwest.

Memorial Day has double potential: one is the outdoors and a display suggesting picnics, barbecues and everything from paper plates to charcoal starter. The other is do-it-yourself. This long weekend is a peak time for painting, wallpapering and small remodeling jobs. Make sure your store develops promotions and displays that say "We understand your wants and needs."

June: Father's Day. Search your stock for products that will please a grandfather as well as a young father in his 20's. Clothing, hobbies, sports, hardware, do-it-yourself tools . . . consider a badge or stick-on that says "Certified to Please" or some such. Again, use signs to tell customers "Remember, Father's Day is June XX." Look for signing opportunities in the graduation gift area.

Promote flags the first two weeks—before Flag Day.

July: Independence Day, picnics, sales and clearances. July 1 is Canada's Dominion Day and July 14 is Bastille Day in France. Consider your county fairs and state fairs—is there a tie-in? "Blue Ribbon Sale" is a possibility. "Grand Prize Sale" with a drawing for a prize? It's a red, white and blue time of year. Sign as if you were having an event—you can tie a loose bunch of sales and clearances into something more exciting to the customer.

August: back-to-school promotions. School-bus yellow. Crayola green and orange. The beginning of fall and fall colors. Don't forget back-to-college—a whole area of need for everything from microwaves (and popcorn) to ironing boards, irons and all that sound equipment. Now it's computers, too. Don't stick entirely with traditional grade school colors. Consider neon, or the biggest fall color trend in apparel. Avoid negative comments about back-to-school, and you'll avoid negative feedback from school executives. Stay upbeat about school.

September: the reality of back to school. Spring colors look wrong. Fall colors look right. Members of the family overlooked in the back-to-school rush want something for themselves. What can you do for mom, dad, and the baby? It's a traditional Baby Sale time. Add toddlers and pre-school children.

September 1 is Mexican Independence Day and fiesta time. Rosh Hashanah starts. And Labor Day is another "Honey

do" weekend of do-it-yourself projects. Paint sales peak. It's time to introduce leaf baggers to the joys of composting and look for ways to make yard clean-up more ecologically sound. Some states are banning yard wastes in their landfills—an opportunity to show alternatives: compost barrels, compost piles made with inexpensive fencing, etc. Look for help from your local and regional solid waste agencies.

October: Columbus Day. Canada's Thanksgiving. That period between back-to-school and Thanksgiving when it's time to promote. Often the month for a "Harvest of Values" store-wide sale. Halloween and all its candy, decorations, cards and costumes. Don't wait until the last week to promote candy. Start on October 1—parents will eat the first purchase and have to come back for more! October 1, reminder: 85 days till Christmas!

October 12 is Columbus Day . . . soon after is Boss's Day. Columbus Day can be a prime promotional event in some markets—in others it's meaningless. Boss's Day could be the trigger for an amusing promotion—after all, who is the boss? And why not suggest that bosses get something for themselves?

November: gear up for Christmas. Thanksgiving promotions. Pray for good winter weather to get all that winter merchandise going! Have signs and quickie displays ready to take advantage of the weather: umbrellas, snowboots, snow shovels, battery cables, winter sunglasses. Watch the weather!

November 2 is All Soul's Day for your Hispanic customers. November 20 is Mexico's Anniversary of Revolution.

Take advantage of your normal store traffic— use signs as advertising.

December: look for Hanukkah on your calendar and make sure you have your presentations ready for the giving that's traditional on that holiday. It's time to deck the halls with ivy, holly and red ribbons. Look for service opportunities like pre-wrapped gifts, displayed and signed at high-traffic points. Monitor your signing and displays almost hourly—keep promotions stocked.

Mexico's Our Lady of Guadalupe's Day is December 12.

Grocery stores have another opportunity to create gift baskets of prepared foods and utensils, highlighting high-margin, premium packages. The box could be as simple as a bakery white box, lined with florist paper. Inside: a cracker assortment, a can of pate, a jar of caviar, several small jars of appetizers. You could add non-alcoholic champagne or, where laws permit, the real thing. These gift boxes are easy to assemble and can be done to order. If any are left after New Year's, their parts can be put back on the shelf. These gift ideas become customer services—gift idea-starters that take advantage of your normal store traffic. You don't have to advertise them—just sign them well.

The week between Christmas and New Year's, look for opportunities to appeal to people who have new "Christmas money." Organize for prompt and efficient handling of returns. Use signs to tell customers how to make returns. Use signs to tempt them with new merchandise and highlight timely markdowns on the old. Organize a presentation of needs for New Year's entertaining.

Happy New Year! It's time to review all of last year's events, take out the old and tired, and insert the new. Start all over again!

Don't Forget Your Local/Regional Sports Activities Calendar!

There is another cycle in the year: the annual cycle of national sports activities and local school sports.

Consider the possibilities in the annual transition from basketball to softball to baseball to summer athletics to soccer to football and hockey. Each team sport has its equipment, its school colors, its organizational uniforms, its after-game celebrations. How involved are you? Do you promote the school colors before homecoming? Are school colors and mascots part of your back-to-school efforts?

For many stores, this cycle can become an important series of events. By using signs to highlight these activities, you show your awareness and involvement in the lives of your customers. Such signs say "We understand you and your life" and "We care."

The idea can be this simple: let's say that your school colors are red and black. Collect your spectator sportswear and accessories in those basic colors; present them with signs that point out this season's "winning colors." You will stimulate sales for what would otherwise be considered basic merchandise, if it were mixed in with your usual assortments.

Use a sports tie-in as the basis for a whimsical sale event—offer 10% off anything in your store that is in your school's colors.

Look for school events and exploit their potential. While sports have all those good qualities of competition, winning, and school spirit . . . there may also be musical or theatrical events, annual art competitions, and don't forget graduation. Also, think about that important week when businesses visit colleges to interview seniors. (And those seniors want to look polished and professional.) It's an untapped reservoir of opportunities. ◆

9. Signs to Help Your Employees and Improve Customer Service

GOOD SIGNING DOESN'T STOP AT THE SELLING FLOOR. There are opportunities to make your stockrooms more efficient, your employee lounge more appealing, and to make you and your employees more effective.

Always greet the customer.

Always look them in the eye.

Always ask if you can help.

REMEMBER:

a SMILE
and a cheerful attitude
are part of your uniform

First, Check Your Stockrooms for Opportunities

Signing stock shelves with the department name and number helps employees find the right area to begin their search for specific merchandise. Keep in mind that usually, a salesperson is looking for something *the customer wants right now*. The faster the salesperson can find the product, the sooner the customer is satisfied. It will pay off in service to look for opportunities to make stock-finding easier.

Stockrooms can be a threatening trip for new employees, particularly the part-timers you hire for peak selling periods like pre-Christmas. Everybody is in a rush and stores sometimes change policies for the season. Free gift boxes, for instance, may be available only at Christmas time. When a salesperson runs out of a particular size and needs one, how easy is it to find in your stockroom, especially when you remember that a customer is waiting? If you stock gift boxes

Stockrooms can be a threatening trip for new employees, particularly the part-timers you hire for peak selling periods like Christmas.

for the holidays, sorting them *by use* and signing them will help many harried salespeople select the right size for the gifts in their department. You'll save money and give better service.

If you are a small-size operation, how do you handle reorders? Do you have a process whereby whoever takes the last item off the stockroom shelf marks it for reorder? *Sign your procedure,* have a clipboard with the proper form for identifying the product and tie a pencil to it. This may not be a perfect system, but it could help you improve your in-stock position.

Second, Sign Your Employee Lounge

Every employee lounge should have two bulletin boards capable of handling the store's current advertising, employment rules and regulations as required by federal and state governments, employee bits of news ("It's a girl!") which draw interest, and space for special employee training messages.

If you have an overriding theme such as, "The customer is always right"—make sure that theme is signed on the back of every stockroom door and in any area frequented by employees. (I have seen such signs in the employees' ladies' room, but perhaps that is going too far?) If you are running a United Way campaign, sign your efforts and update them. If you are running a sales contest, sign the effort and keep updates coming.

Store personnel in large chains are inundated with memos, directives and changes. If you can turn that memo or request into a sign, you have created a "poster" or "telegram" which has a much better chance of being read—and read by everyone including the part-time help. Store personnel in small stores have the opposite problem: they rarely get any formal information at all. "Tele-grammed" training messages can get their attention, in the lounge and background areas of your store.

Third, Sign Special Situations

When inventory time comes around—check to see what your stores are doing to pre-pare for it—and see if your sign shop can't improve the system. This is using signing strictly internally, but it can be of enor-mous help in facilitating work done primarily by part-timers and always under time pressure.

Help Wanted

HELP WANTED

★ Day cashier
★ $6.00/hr. to start
★ Store discounts
★ Flexible hours

When you are looking for part-time help, do you have a hand-made sign that hangs forlornly in the window and says, "HELP WANTED"—or is your sign made the same way as your display signing? One looks cheap, one looks profes-sional. Which way would you rather look?

Fourth, Sign Your Training Tips

Refresh your employee signing on a regular basis by rotating through your training policies, emphasizing one each month, for instance:

Tip of the month:

START A SMILE!

PASS ON A SMILE!

The concept is: use signs to improve employees' ability to give good service. Help *them* find merchandise faster and easier. Help *them* understand and remember your important policies. Remind *them* that you want "service with a smile."

With good, professionally printed signs, you will be communicating professionally. Quickly. Economically.

Check your back rooms, your receiving area, your employee lounge, your stockrooms for opportunities.

Merchandise returns are an opportunity to correct a problem.

Be nice. Help the customer. When a return is hassle-free, the customer will remain a customer.

We need customers!

Fifth, Don't Overlook the Benefits of Store Signing to Your Employees

When a product is well signed, it becomes a back-up for the salesperson. Signs are the "silent salespeople" that can tell the customer what is most important about each product. Salespeople are freed from repetitive or obvious questions and can concentrate on closing sales and giving faster service. In many cases, customer questions can be answered by simply referring to the sign. I have seen a salesperson literally read the product's benefits off the sign, to the customer, and have the customer satisfied enough to buy the product. I have been in a store's television department and been able to help a customer find the right TV set, because the signing pointed out the important hidden benefit: the sets with earphone capabilities. On the other hand, an aggressive salesperson can't over promise or mislead the customer, because the sign is there with the facts. Professional signing adds to the ambiance of your store and makes your employees feel better and act better. Studies show that printed signs establish the price: customers believe that hand-printed price signs mean that the items will be marked down further or that the price is negotiable. Printed signs get respect—by your employees as well as customers. ◆

10. 65 Signs and How to Improve Them

REVERSE LETTERS ARE PARTICULARLY EFFECTIVE for your general "sale" or "clearance" messages, separating them from your product headline. If possible, regular pricing should show single (each) price and the multiple that matches your feature. In this case, "Reg. 2/1.18" could be the first of the three benefits. Always do the math for the customer if you can.

CLEARANCE

GAS LINE ANTI-FREEZE

Reg. 59¢
12-oz. size

● Fuel system dryer
● Takes the water out
● While supplies last

2/.90

Right: here is the same product signed in a portrait or vertical version. Putting the regular price line in a different typeface helps catch your eye. The use of Heet (national brand) improves the headline.

Below, right: same copy in a 5¹/₂ x 7″ size sign. With the proper equipment you *can* get benefits on small signs, suitable for gondola runs. The large price indicates value. Without the Clearance header, this could be a good format to show value at regular price, too. Copy point: "While supplies last" isn't necessary with a clearance heading. It is understood by customers when they see the word "Clearance."

Below: a printed, small 3¹/₂ x 5¹/₂″ size sign still communicates. It's clean, effective and won't detract from the merchandise. The use of the specific size of Heet (12 ounces) is important. It may be on the shelf next to a larger size that is not on clearance.

SPECIAL

Heet ANTI-FREEZE

- Fuel system dryer
- Takes the water out
- 12-ounce size

Reg. 59¢

2/.90

CLEARANCE

GAS LINE ANTI-FREEZE

Reg. 59¢
12-oz. size

- Fuel system dryer
- Takes the water out
- While supplies last

2/.90

CLEARANCE

GAS LINE ANTI-FREEZE

Reg. 59¢
12-oz. size

- Fuel system dryer
- Takes the water out
- While supplies last

2/.90

Right: three simple feature comments. This could be used effectively when you have several models and want to set up a "good, better, best" arrangement and help trade the customer up. Use of model number on equipment like this helps clarify the offer and, in self-service environments, helps the customer find the right boxed merchandise.

Below: note that this is not a sale offer, yet this sign sells garden hose by giving all the benefits concisely and emphasizing its price. The use of a 99¢ price ending could be a regular price to some discounters, and a sale price to some department stores which usually have 95¢ price endings. Your store needs a price policy to clarify, internally as well as to customers, what's going on. This should not be left to the discretion of department managers.

Toro Mower

☞ **Self-propelled**
☞ **21"-wide cut**
☞ **Model #21-4270**

Reg. $289 **$199**

SWAN HOSE

● **5/8" diam., 50' length**
● **Nylon reinforced**
● **10-year warranty**

15.99

Right: note the less bold type face. Its lighter weight (thickness) makes it more appealing in a fashion department. If the brand name helps, use it. In fact, you might want to reverse the copy to say "Gitano" first and then "Clearance."

Below: "Assorted colors" says nothing. "Price good through Wednesday" says a lot. (On Thursday, be sure to take down the sign!) Again, you could say "Gitano Sale" and emphasize brand first. If "Sale" is preprinted on the sign, it works better set in reverse type, like the signs on page 106.

CLEARANCE
GITANO

- Ladies' casuals
- Prewashed
- 100% cotton

$ **26** ⁹⁵

SALE

GITANO

- Ladies' cool casuals
- Comfortable cotton knits
- Prewashed and preshrunk
- Reinforced stitching on seams
- Assorted colors
- Price good through Wednesday
- Limit: 4 per customer

$ **26** ⁹⁵

Right: leading with the designer name is a good idea. Using the product benefits space to reinforce one of your store's services is an excellent idea, too.

Below: "Save $10" would be much more powerful than "Tough as the game." Eliminate the meaningless "many colors and patterns." Don't add copy just to fill the space.

Bill Blass
Silk Scarves

- Solids, patterns, stripes
- Great gift idea
- FREE gift wrapping!

$22⁰⁰

"Tough as the game ..."
Rugby Shirts

- 100% cotton
- Wrinkle resistant
- Machine washable
- Many colors and patterns
- Sizes S, M, L, and XL

29.50

Regular $39.50

Stonewashed denim

Levi's 501

- Cool, comfortable cotton
- Extremely durable
- Waists 29 - 40
- Inseams 28 - 38
- Save $10 today!

21.95

Regular $31.95

Holiday Sale!

SEPARATES

- Resist wrinkles
- Perfect for travel
- 55% linen, 45% polyester

Jackets $98   **Pants $65**

Left: the $10 off is a primary (and temporary) benefit. It should be above "Levi's 501." But which style is the 501? Boot leg or tapered? Button fly or zip? The first benefit could be "stonewashed cotton denim." Then describe what makes this Levi a 501. The size offering should be matched with individual size signs or labels, with merchandise organized by size.

Below: fabric content is important for today's shopper. The benefit, "Perfect for travel" is a cliche and not believable. Nothing is perfect! It would be better to give some washability claim, or support the "resists wrinkles" claim somehow.

Right: here, when you're in the ladies' shoe department, it would be more effective to have "Clearance" in bigger, bolder type, and the "ladies' shoes" smaller or not there at all. "Many styles and colors" says nothing. Cut it.

Below: standard, basic and powerful sign. The use of reverse type is a good way to separate a "Special" from a "Sale" or "Clearance." But all three can be formatted alike, with different colors used to pre-print the reverse type.

CLEARANCE!
LADIES' SHOES

- Many styles and colors
- Flats, sandals & heels
- Everything MUST GO

$19.95/Pair

SPECIAL
25%
off marked price

Right: while the use of a border can suggest an event, better to follow this maxim: if it doesn't contribute to communication, leave it out. White space can be just as effective and may be more effective on this sign. Underlining here is a good idea. It can work if done with a light hand. "While available" is a questionable call to action and it suffers from being positioned at the end. ("One size fits most while available"?) Put it first or say "No rainchecks." Note capital "A" in "All." Use typical sentence structure to avoid deciding what to capitalize, or cap the beginning of every line and no more. "One size fits most" is certainly more believable than "One size fits *all.*"

Is this a sale? Probably not, but these shirts are an excellent value and deserve a large feature price. Note the lighter type for an apparel item versus hardware or food.

Here Comes Winter

SALE

Ladies'
Multi-color, All-wool
SWEATERS

One size fits most
While available

21.00

15.99

Cotton Dress Shirts

● Hand-stitched seams
● Regular or tapered styling
● Solids, checks & pinstripes

Mail these cards!

Please take a moment to complete the postpaid return card below. We'd like your reactions to "Signs That Sell," and your ideas on how to improve it!

And to find out how the innovative Impulse Sign System can help you make great-looking signs right in your store, send in the bottom postcard. We want to hear from you!

Let us know . . .

what you think of this edition of "Signs That Sell." We'd like your questions, comments, suggestions, even case histories --- anything that will help us make future editions of this handbook even better.

_____

_____

_____

_____

_____

Thank You!

insignia® systems, inc.
10801 Red Circle Drive
Minnetonka, MN 55343

Make great-looking signs in seconds. Anyone can do it . . . on Impulse®!

The Impulse Sign System automatically lays out, typesets, and prints professional-quality signs. . .in seconds. It produces any size up to 11″ x 14″, and uses no inks, ribbons, or toner. Predesigned formats and special cardweight sign stock mean absolutely ANYONE can make great-looking signs, without training. And we can preprint your logo, sales event, etc. onto sign cards for a truly custom look. For a FREE sample sign, mail this card, or call **1-800-874-4648.**

Name _____

Store _____

Address _____

City
State, Zip _____

Phone ( ) _____

BUSINESS REPLY MAIL
FIRST-CLASS MAIL   PERMIT NO. 1852   MINNETONKA, MN

POSTAGE WILL BE PAID BY ADDRESSEE

insignia® systems, inc.
10801 Red Circle Drive
Minnetonka, MN 55343-9734

Name _____

Store _____

Address _____

City
State, Zip _____

Phone ( ) _____

BUSINESS REPLY MAIL
FIRST-CLASS MAIL   PERMIT NO. 1852   MINNETONKA, MN

POSTAGE WILL BE PAID BY ADDRESSEE

insignia® systems, inc.
10801 Red Circle Drive
Minnetonka, MN 55343-9734

Right: never try to translate jargon or special lingo into type. It's difficult to read and isn't your voice. Keep your own language. A sign is *you* talking. In this case, "Just do it" may work, to remind customers of Nike television advertising and its emotional pull.

Center: here, "Buy three pair, get the fourth FREE" is buried. It should be featured. This is a good sales technique for an item frequently purchased in multiples. The sign at bottom is a better, clearer offer.

93.50

Nike "Air Jordans"

- Patented air pillow in sole
- High-top styling is what's hap'nin'
- JUST DO IT

3.25/Pair

Burlington Socks
- Reinforced heel and toe
- Choose crew length or mid calf
- Buy three pair, get the fourth FREE

3.25/Pair

4 Pair for 9.75

(Like getting the 4th pair FREE!)
- Burlington CREW or Mid-Calf
- Reinforced heel and toe

169.00

London Fog Trench Coats

- Water-repellent cotton duck
- With zip-in, zip-out winter lining
- Sizes S - M - L

Left: there are two good, unobvious benefits here. Sell what they can't see.

Center: good basic sign summarizes the brands and merchandise on sale. A more powerful second line would be "Save 7.00 to 12.05." Always spell out savings if you can. And when does this sale end?

Below: this might be a good sign at the front of the store or in the window, to give customers some idea of your assortment and pricing. It says you have brands for the whole family. An improvement would be to separate the listings by "kids," "women's shoes" and "men's shoes." Always help the customer shop your sign as well as your store. They're busy.

Athletic Shoes
for the whole family

New Balance Swifts	Reg. 49.95	$38.95
Nike Sportsters	Reg. 43.95	$33.95
Puma Soccer Shoes	Reg. 52.95	$41.95
Reebok Workouts	Reg. 39.95	$30.95
Converse Youth	Reg. 29.95	$22.95
L.A. Gear Malibu	Reg. 52.00	$39.95

Athletic Shoes
for the whole family

New Balance Swifts	$38.95
Nike Sportsters	$33.95
Puma Soccer Shoes	$41.95
Reebok Workouts	$29.95
Converse Youth	$32.95
L.A. Gear Malibu	$39.95
El Tigré Clawtracks	$33.00
Converse All-Star	$25.90
Reebok Magic	$69.95
Nike Air Jordan	$97.50
Wilson ProCourt	$67.00
Slazenger Champ	$72.50

Right: this sign makes good use of a primary, important feature. Even though it is legally necessary for all kids' sleepers to be flame retardant, it doesn't hurt to use it as a benefit sometimes. Many products have this type of emotional feature. Use it, especially if it's newsworthy. Your sign messages can gain strength by reinforcing local or national concerns.

Below: typical seafood sign. Reverse lettering message, "Today's Catch" implies a special price or a special fresh offering. The brush-type font emulates handwriting yet is clear enough to handle all the information and benefits.

Kids' Sleepwear

All with flame-retardant fabric

Bart Simpson P.J.'s	Sizes 4-14	Reg. 14.99	12.00
Nintendo Pajamas	Sizes 4-14	Reg. 14.00	12.99
Ghost Busters P.J.'s	Sizes 4-7	Reg. 16.00	13.99
Looney Tunes 'Jams	Sizes 4-7	Reg. 12.00	9.99
G.I. Joe Pullover	Sizes 4-14	Reg. 15.00	11.99
Smurfs Shortsleeve	Sizes 6-14	Reg. 16.00	12.99
Ninja Turtles	Sizes 4-7	Reg. 14.99	12.99
Dick Tracy Yellows	Sizes 4-7	Reg. 15.99	13.00

TODAY'S CATCH

FRESH
WALLEYE
PIKE
FILLETS

$3.99 lb.

THIS WEEK'S SPECIAL

LETTUCE

59¢ head

Left: identify all your specials with signs. Take advantage of any unusually good shipment. Your "special" could be items with a slightly higher margin for you. Pricing by "head" or item versus price per pound is a service to the customer.

Below: occasionally a "given," like freshness for produce, can work with repetition.

FRESH! FRESH! FRESH!

PAPAYAS

99¢ each

Right: this simple sign is well organized and effective. It says where the spinach was grown, the package size and the regular price. "Washed" is a big benefit.

Below: a 60¢ bargain (actually 20% off)! In this case the brand name is probably most important. But "Save 60¢" might be as newsworthy as "Cored FREE."

CALIFORNIA
WASHED
SPINACH

Reg. 2.89

$2^{\underline{39}}$

16-oz. pkg.

DEL MONTE
PINEAPPLE

Reg. 2.99

$2^{\underline{39}}$

Cored FREE

HOMEGROWN
CANTALOUPE
1 69
FRESH
TODAY
Each

Left: "Homegrown" supports "Fresh today" and is used appropriately. Also good are phrases like "Just arrived."

Below: this is a good way to make the customers aware of your new produce items. A grocer's maxim: the more they buy early in the season, the more they will buy all season long. Using a "First of the season special" format will work as long as you police its use and don't allow the sign to stay up any longer than two weeks. "First of" is preferred to "First o' "—avoid playing with the language.

FIRST O' THE SEASON SPECIAL
BLUEBERRIES
99 ¢
Save
40¢
Pint
Carton

Right: here is a good multiple-selling opportunity. Having three to choose from and at a 3/ price looks like a friendly service. Do this in the department, never at checkout where you don't want any "which ones" decision-making delays.

Below, right: don't be afraid to go to higher multiples in pricing if you can hit a "magic" or reasonable total price. Here, one dollar seems very reasonable. You can almost hear the customer say, "Might as well."

Below, left: the key in multiple-pricing is to hit an easy to understand price point. Even dollar amounts are ideal. The "stock up" supporting line is good; it adds a reason why to the multiple pricing. However, the sale savings are obscure. What would the 3/ *regular price* be? If you don't get those details on the sign, the customer can stand and wonder—and leave without buying.

CANDY BARS

3/1⁰⁰

SNICKERS, M & M's, HERSHEY'S

KOOL - AID

6/1⁰⁰

oose from 12 delicious flavors!

PEPSI & DIET PEPSI

3/5⁰⁰

Stock up on Sale-Priced 6-Packs!

TOMATO SOUP

4/1⁰⁰

Flavorite Brand   **10-oz cans**

LEAN GROUND BEEF

For burgers, sloppy joes, meatballs!

4 lb /3⁸⁹

Left: many grocers forget to sign their own private brands. Since most private brands are more profitable than name brands, it will pay to look for opportunities—multiple-pricing opportunities, too. Here, 4/$1.00 is reasonably simple to divide and find an "each" price, yet to be absolutely sure, a "25¢ each" wouldn't hurt.

Below, left: even a staple basic can be signed to enhance the offering. Use serving suggestions, directions and menu additions as often as possible. If you're really into service, you would offer the calorie count per unit of each style of ground beef you offer. Or some sort of fat content comparison.

Below: complete information, such as nutritional values, provides great customer service. Give your customers more reasons to buy . . . and more will!

everyday discount price

A great source of Vitamin B6!

BANANAS

1 medium-size (3.5 oz.) has:
Calories: **70**
Dietary Fiber: **1 gram**

A tasty way to get Vitamins C and A, as well as Potassium, Phosphorus and Calcium.

Low Sodium ● Low Fat
Cholesterol Free

39¢

Per Lb.

Right: excellent benefits, but what is for $2.99—a pint, quart or half gallon? Don't overlook the basics, while striving for romance.

Below, right: "Two pounds for $3.74, regularly 2/$4.98" would be more powerful than the second package half-price which is buried in the benefits. Savings should *always* be the feature. If, for special reasons, you don't want to mark down the first package, and only want a "second package" price cut—get it up front—feature the offer.

Below, left: Quick: what is half of $3.59? Do you really want to try to do the math while you're shopping the frozen food section? It is easy to add "$1.80 each" after the last benefit— 12-ounce size. When you don't put the single price on the sign, the customer can feel like he or she is being forced to buy more than one—and resent it.

2.99
Ben & Jerry's Ice Cream

- 100% pure ingredients
- Actually mixed by Ben & Jerry
- Choose from 7 fabulous flavors

2.49
Oscar Mayer Bacon

- Healthier! Lower salt, less fat
- One-pound package
- Second package half-price

2/3.59
Stouffer's Pizza

- Made with real cheese
- Microwavable…ready in 5 minutes!
- Sausage, Pepperoni, or Combo
- 12-ounce size

Right: this sign does a beginner's job of influencing the customer to buy. It has more enthusiasm than facts. Having recipes available and mentioning "free recipe with purchase" or "take our special recipe" would help overcome fears about being too adventurous!

Below, right: every grocery store with a yogurt machine should have a simple but effective information sign. This sign doesn't answer several important questions. First question: what's the price of the basic yogurt? Second question: are the toppings complimentary? Or 25¢ each? Price is important! No price on the sign implies they are free.

8.29

Fresh Live Lobster

- Flown in daily from New England
- Easy to prepare…just steam and serve with butter!
- Turn an ordinary dinner into an adventure!

YOGURT CONE TOPPINGS

CANDY SPRINKLES

HOT FUDGE

CARAMEL SAUCE

NUTS

TOFFEE CRUNCH

PINEAPPLE

CHOCOLATE CHIPS

PEANUT BUTTER CHIPS

M & M's

Right: a food summary sign can be useful for the price comparison shoppers. Again, organization of any kind will help. Start with the cheapest item and go up to the most expensive. The "Ground Sirloin" should be first on this sign. And actual savings might help. "Save 0 to 00¢" is good, but not if you had to cut the "Sale on all" line. Putting *all* the entrees on sale is an excellent benefit to the customer.

Below, right: several items at the same sale price can be very effective. "Prices slashed" implies a large markdown. If so, "Save 0 to 00" might be stronger. Be specific when savings are significant. Use percentages if they sound like more.

Below: with the right sign-making equipment, everything is possible. In dead space, the "stock up for gifts" is a good rationalization for the customer and doesn't detract from the sign.

Lean Cuisine

Sale on all Heat n' Eat Entrees

● Chicken Kiev	Reg. 3.29	2.49
● Beef Stroganoff	Reg. 3.39	2.49
● Spaghetti	Reg. 2.99	2.29
● Sirloin Tips	Reg. 3.59	2.79
● Veal Parmesan	Reg. 3.29	2.49
● Ground Sirloin	Reg. 2.89	2.29

PRICES SLASHED

- Sunbeam Toaster
- G.E. Fry Pan
- Oster Blender
- Corning Warmer
- Krups Percolator

Your Choice

29⁸⁷

PRICES SLASHED

● **Sunbeam Toaster**
● **G.E. Fry Pan**
● **Oster Blender**
● **Mr. Coffee - Coffee Maker**

Your Choice

29⁸⁸

Stock up for gifts!

HOUSEWARES SALE

- Hamilton Beach Can Opener
- Oster Fry Daddy
- Hoover Mini-Vac
- Corningware Hotplate

Take Your Pick!

19⁷⁹

Values to $29

Holiday Savings

- Aqua Net Hair Spray
- Crest Toothpaste (7-oz.)
- Maybelline Nail Files
- Head & Shoulders (travel size)
- Sure Deodorant (travel size)

Stock Up at this Super Price

99¢

Left: "Values to $29" is not acceptable to most States' Attorneys General. Lowest to highest savings should be mentioned. "Save $11 to $29" is correct.

Below, left: "Holiday" savings may be confusing with this assortment. These are travel items and sizes. Call them "Travel" or "Vacation" specials.

Below: this sign will work in front of a large assortment of baseball gloves where it is clear what merchandise is on special. You have to read a bit to discover that the sign is talking about baseball gloves. "All-star specials" may be a good handle for a sporting goods store. But where is the urgency to buy? How long will this special be in force?

ALL-STAR SPECIALS

- ★ Mizuno Josè Canseco glove
- ★ Rawlings Kirby Puckett model
- ★ Wilson Bob Uecker catcher's mitt
- ★ Spalding Wade Boggs autograph
- ★ MacGregor Ozzie Smith model

Your Choice

29⁸⁸

Right: this sign is attractively laid out and uses a good crisp typeface. The heavy bullets lead the eye down the reasons to buy. The "Four built-in speakers" gives a hidden benefit. However, is "The sharpest picture" believable and a proven fact? "Save $400" should be at the top of the sign! And "SALE", too. Savings first!

Below: to pick a few nits here: you "save on" and have a "sale of." Using a command verb such as "Save on the classics" is stronger. This sign is a good idea. You rarely see multiple pricing in bookstores. Adding an "each" price would be helpful. The customer doesn't have to stop and do the math to figure out the cost for only one—or maybe four or five books!

Television as it was meant to be…

Mitsubishi 35"

- The sharpest picture available in any size
- Attractive black cabinetry with casters
- Four built-in Concertsound speakers
- Save $400 off the regular price

$2195

A Sale of The Classics!

Book Sale

- ☞ **"Last of the Mohicans"**
- ☞ **Melville's "Moby Dick"**
- ☞ **"Gone With the Wind"**
- ☞ **"The Scarlet Letter"**
- ☞ **"Brothers Karamazov"**
- ☞ **"The Grapes of Wrath"**
- ☞ **"The Glass Menagerie"**
- ☞ **"Little Women"**

3/19.95

"Spruce up" your yard ...

Perennials

- Garden Mum (sun)
- Bleeding Heart (sun)
- Snow on the Mountain
- Hardy Ferns (shade)
- Daisy (sun)

99¢/Pack

Ornamentals, shade, fruit

TREE SALE

☞ Sugar Maple (8-ft.)
☞ Black Walnut (8-ft.)
☞ Weeping Willow (6-ft.)
☞ Flowering Crab (8-ft.)
☞ Russian Olive (6-ft.)

$39.99

Left: "Spruce up" your yard is a meaningless pun and not necessary. The gardener is already in the department looking for plants. Service and savings signing copy is the ultimate. This sign could be organized by "sun" and "shade." For instance:

> Garden Mum,
> Bleeding Heart,
> and Daisy for sun
> Snow on the Mountain,
> Hardy Ferns for shade

Below, left: by combining ornamental, shade and fruit trees on one sign, you have a mishmash. Better to cut the introductory line and put in the amount of money saved during this sale.

The fact that these are larger-size trees could be the basis for a more powerful revision of this sign, too.

Right: the more reasons to buy, the better. Even on a small sign, here are six good reasons to buy. And one good reason to buy three! Suggestion: Take out "Beautiful spring flowers" (almost everyone knows what a lilac looks like), and put the "Buy 3, get one FREE" copy up there at the top, where it's read first.

Below: an unusual combination value sign. Note use of "stars" as bullet points. They soften the effect. Somewhere, each item should also be signed. This may not look like a value to you, but the inexperienced camper may say, "Gee, we could get equipped for under $300." At your store, of course.

Beautiful spring flowers

PINK LILAC

- ● Fast, compact growth
- ● Prunes to any shape
- ● Fabulous fall color
- ● Grows in sun or shade
- ● Perfect hedge, accent
- ● Guaranteed to grow
- ● Buy 3, get one FREE!

$8.99

12-piece Deluxe

Tent Package

- ★ 9' x 11' Dome Tent
- ★ 4 folding stools
- ★ 8-pc. cook set
- ★ Propane lantern
- ★ Propane stove
- ★ 2 sleeping bags
- ★ 2 air matresses

$299⁰⁰

BATTERY

SALE

- Cadmium-Plus technology
- 575 cold-cranking amps
- Maintenance-free
- Streamlined size
- 60-month warranty
- Fits all cars and pick-ups

42.95

Collector's Edition Knives

WOW!

- High-carbon steel
- Damascus style blade
- Exotic wood handles
- Includes display box

79.95

Left: here's a strong, bold look. Good use of layout and typeface. Six benefits enhance the perceived value.

Below: if you are excited about your item or its price, let your customers know it. Enthusiasm sells. Just don't do it too often.

Right: this sign is not as good as it could be. What's missing? Weatherproof? Size availability? Hidden features? Maybe this item doesn't need any sign at all.

Below: feature/benefits do sell products, even commodity appliances. It also helps the customer decide between products on your shelves.

$69.00

Satin Jacket

- Nylon shell
- Polyester fiberfill
- Snap-front closures

199.99

Sanyo Microwave

✓ Rack for 2-level cooking
✓ 10 power levels for ccoking versatility
✓ Special "Quik-Defrost" feature

Right: this sign makes good use of the brand name and the easily compared regular price column. Again, go from lowest price to highest price—don't let items appear at random on any sort of list. Organize, organize, organize.

Below: "All gold" is too general. Is it pure gold or all your gold jewelry? (See how easy it is to inadvertently mislead the customer?) Is it all 14K? That's most important. Since gold jewelry is discounted so heavily, you need to be more price-specific to get the customers' attention. What is each piece's regular price and sale price?

Oneida Flatware

Quality Stainless...5-pc. settings

Pattern	Regular	SALE
Golden Accents	75.00	49.99
Heirloom Ltd.	75.00	49.99
Satinique	40.00	29.99
Chateau	30.00	19.99

ONE-DAY SALE!

All Gold Jewelry

- 14K Heart Cobra Chain
- Ridged Swirl Button Earrings
- 14K Twisted Rope Chain
- 14K Three-plus-One Link Chain
- Ladies' Nameplate Necklace
- Men's 3-Initial Tie Tack
- Men's 8-inch Name Bracelet
- Triple Herringbone Chain

Bra and Bikini sets

Cotton and nylon

White, black, or nude

$15.00 set

Left: watch out for terms like "nude" which can offend minorities. Just whose color "nude" will you use? Always check for the unexpected term that can be offensive.

Center: any sign that starts with the word "NO" is a customer turn-off. Try to find a positive.

Below: this sign is much friendlier, and turns the store policy into a customer benefit.

NO RETURNS WITHOUT RECEIPTS

SAVE YOUR RECEIPTS

In case you want to return your purchase, we must have a receipt. This policy is necessary for us to bring you our low prices.

Right: whew! What can you say about this? Better to state the policy—give customers a reason for anything that might sound negative. ◆

NO RETURNS ON BATHING SUITS

NO RETURNS ON UNDERWEAR

BE SURE IT FITS

According to federal law, we cannot accept a return on underwear or swimwear.

11. Sales, Clearances and Special Purchases —How to Stay Out of Trouble

WHEN YOU ARE SIGNING A PRICE BREAK on any merchandise, it is important to know the rules and regulations of your state government and the local Better Business Bureaus. Because of past abuses, they are particularly attentive to how retailers announce price promotions—and how they execute them.

33% off is an excellent promotion. Note that the store did everything via signs to make buying easier for the customer. Each style rake has a sign indicating regular and sale price.

A "Sale" Means . . .

. . . this piece of merchandise is temporarily marked down in price. Many states require a minimum of 5% markdown to make it a "sale." The merchandise should have been offered for sale *and sold significantly* at the regular price, two weeks to 30 days (state rules vary on this) before it is offered for sale, if you are using a "regular price" as a comparative.

It is only a "regular price" if it has *sold* at a regular price. Any state's Attorney General can ask you for sales information regarding regular selling price, once you have quoted it in a sale ad. If you have not sold a "significant amount" at regular price, you can be prosecuted.

This law resulted from so many retailers quoting false "regular" prices, and offering the public 25% and 50% off "regular" prices when the "regular" prices never existed.

One deviation from the rule is an "introductory price." You can lower the price during the

The term "sale" was misused so much . . . . that many federal and state rules were put in place to protect the consumer.

introduction of a product, *if* you raise the price following the introductory period, for 30 days.

The term "sale" was misused so much during the freewheeling days in the 1960's and "B.A."—before activists, that many federal and state rules were put in place to protect the consumer. For instance, a "going out of business sale" is so strictly regulated in some states that you must literally be out of business within 30 days from the first statement. This is so stringent that the informal announcement or "rumor" that you are going out of business can be construed as the first knowledge of it, and you *have* to be out of business 30 days hence. This law started in New York, where shops were "going out of business" on busy New York City streets—for years! Retail outlaws, unfortunately, created detailed and binding laws for the lawful. Consult your state's Attorney General's office before you begin any such action. And be extra careful about announcing any "liquidation sale" of a small part of your business, or as an end-of-season clearance—if it is construed as going out of business, you may inadvertently get into trouble with your state laws on this subject.

A "Clearance" Means . . .

. . . simply that you are marking down the merchandise for the season and it will not be marked up again. This is a most attractive term for the customer. The smart shopper understands that this is *your* merchandise, regularly purchased and held in stock. It hasn't been brought in for a sale. It is a *bona fide bargain.* Clearance racks are irresistible. Often the racks contain trend merchandise too far forward for the general public, so the trend shopper understands it and gets a great bargain. The racks can contain mislabeled merchandise—the wrong sizing, or something too slim on top and big on the bottom and *just right* for the customer. Or it simply contains incredible bargains at the end of the season. In any event, "CLEARANCE" is a wonderful word and should be used whenever it is credible.

CLEARANCE

Velour jogging suits

50% off

CLEARANCE

Velour jogging suits

Originally $100.00

NOW $50.00

Interim markdowns have been taken

If interim markdowns have been taken from the original price, you need to say so, only you refer to the original price and the new clearance price.

A "Special Purchase"

. . . can cover a multitude of sins, mostly on the part of manufacturers. A manufacturer may have produced too many of a good item, or a trend is in the peak to post-peak mode and the manufacturer senses a decline in demand for the product. One way to maintain demand or to get rid of current inventory, is to reduce wholesale prices to the retailer. A smart retailer will turn those savings over to the customer, and declare a "special purchase."

This is not a sale because the merchandise cannot always be reordered and rainchecks can't always be honored. It is a deal from the manufacturer, passed on to the customer.

A "special purchase" can also be the tail end of a production line, which is all right if you're dealing in sweaters or skirts, but may not be satisfactory if you are selling electronic products or sound equipment. The reason for the special purchase is really that the *manufacturer* is clearing its product, and it will not be manufactured again. If it will not be manufactured again, and it is an electronic product, it is your responsibility to tell the public so. If it is a simple end-of-line bargain, and the product will be in production again later, that is simply a manufacturer's deal, and all you have to say is "special purchase."

Sometimes a manufacturer cuts the price of its product in order to gain market share or for some competitive reason. That is a "special purchase" or a "sale" depending upon what your marketing aims are. Just be sure you understand whether the product will continue to be manufactured and that you make that clear to your customers.

Here are some examples of promotional signing and what they should mean:

The sign directly below means that the former price, XX.OO, is the actual price that you were offering this merchandise, for a reasonable amount of time (2 weeks to 30 days) and immediately before this offer.

The word "compare" means that you have shopped local competition and have found that principal retail outlets in the market have been selling the *identical* merchandise at XX.OO. It can be phrased "Selling elsewhere," but you better have evidence of this, in case

---

WIDGETS

Regularly XX.00

Now just ZZ.00

This means that the former price, XX.00, is the actual price that you were offering this merchandise, for a reasonable amount of time (2 weeks to 30 days) and immediately before this offer.

WIDGETS

Compare at XX.00

Now just ZZ.00

The word "compare" means that you have shopped local competition and have found that principal retail outlets in the market have been selling the *identical* merchandise at XX.00.

someone from the State Attorney General's office drops in. Legitimate advertisers actually purchase the piece of goods from competition, so they have a sales slip as proof. If the item is easily recognized, and if it is a piece of electronics, for instance, and has a manufacturer's style number or brand name, a competitor's ad can be your proof.

Using "List Price" is slippery. The sign at top right follows the rules because it doesn't promise savings—but it does imply savings. If no one in your trade area is selling Widgets at list price some states will frown on this practice. Note that there is no mention of "Now just" or any phrase that implies you cut the price. You're simply offering manufacturer's list price. As I said, slippery.

The sign at right clearly states that the Widgets are irregular, hence the dramatic drop in price. To stay clearly within the law, don't use the term "regularly" with the comparative—that may imply you sell irregulars at a higher price. It is assumed you are using a comparative price based on perfect Widgets which you have been selling at XX.OO.

WIDGETS
List Price, XX.00

Our Price, ZZ.00

Using "List Price" is slippery. The above sign follows the rules because it doesn't promise savings—but it does imply savings.

WIDGETS
Irregulars
If perfect, XX.00

$ZZ.00

Here, you are clearly stating that the Widgets are irregular, hence the dramatic drop in price.

One of the most difficult disciplines to manage, is to *get the sign down after the sale time limit.* This is important. A three-day sale that goes on for a week tells your customers that they don't have to buy it right away—and your sale messages can lose their sense of urgency. Being honest about the length of the sale is as important as being honest about the comparative prices and quality of the merchandise.

Extra charges should not be hidden in small type. The bottom sign meets the letter of the law, but isn't perfectly clear to the customer. You are running the risk of misleading a customer who reads the feature price and doesn't read the fine print. The sign directly below is more honest. The customer doesn't have to mentally add on assembly charges; everything is clearly spelled out. And there won't be any arguments or confusion at the checkout.

THREE DAY SALE

WIDGETS

ZZ.00

ONE DAY SALE

WIDGETS

ZZ.00

BICYCLES

10-speed

Assembled $179.95

Unassembled $159.95

Extra charges should not be hidden in small type. The sign below meets the letter of the law, but isn't perfectly clear to the customer. The sign above is more honest.

BICYCLES

10-speed

$159.95

Assembly $15.99

A Range of Prices and Savings

It is considered deceptive to state or imply that any products are being offered for sale at a range of prices or at a range of discounts unless the highest price or lowest discount is clearly marked and a reasonable number are offered at that price. A good guide is to offer at least 5% of the items at the largest advertised discount.

Warning!

Sales, Clearances and Special Purchases may be your most-used subjects of signing—yet they may be your least-understood. Since you have an obligation to be honest-dealing and to stay out of trouble with various state and federal oversight organizations, it behooves you to make sure that you and all your associates understand the terms and what each requires. Do not depend 100% on the

SAVE

FROM 10%

Correct but not strong enough.

SAVE UP TO

$100.00

This will be considered misleading and is not recommended.

SAVE

$10 to $30

This is the best, most honest sign. Just be sure you have at least 5% of your stock at the $30 savings level.

SAVE

50% and more!

This is correct, and can motivate a customer to investigate the rack to see what "more" really means. Again, at least 5% of the stock should be "more."

examples in this chapter! Local and state regulations vary. Be sure you have copies of the signing and advertising laws, regulations and directions of your State Attorney General's office.

Mining the Laws for Customer Service

Your customers may not know about your state's consumer-protection laws, or they may want reassurance about the law—and your compliance. Here is an opportunity for benefit signing.

Child sleepwear flammability—if you carry children's wear are you signing your sleepwear as flame retardant?

Automobile car seats and restraints for children—do your products comply and are you informing customers that "it's the law" to have a car seat?

Mattress and upholstered furniture contents—there are benefits in the contents. Make it easy for the customer to find out what he or she is buying.

Unit pricing—if you are a general merchandise store and carry some grocery products, you may be operating under a law that requires unit pricing.

Are you in compliance?

Cities can also have laws governing merchandise. For instance, spray cans of paint are not allowed for sale to minors in some cities; some city garbage facilities demand that all garbage cans be a certain size—or under a specific size. Better that you know the laws and appear helpful rather than sell a product that is illegal.

Does your state have any "lemon laws" that apply to merchandise you sell? Take the law and make it your customer service policy—and sign it. You'll be taking a lemon and making lemonade. ◆

Kids' Sleepwear

All with flame-retardant fabric

Bart Simpson P.J.'s	Sizes 4-14	Reg. 14.99	12.00
Nintendo Pajamas	Sizes 4-14	Reg. 14.00	12.99
Ghost Busters P.J.'s	Sizes 4-7	Reg. 16.00	13.99
Looney Tunes 'Jams	Sizes 4-7	Reg. 12.00	9.99
G.I. Joe Pullover	Sizes 4-14	Reg. 15.00	11.99
Smurfs Shortsleeve	Sizes 6-14	Reg. 16.00	12.99
Ninja Turtles	Sizes 4-7	Reg. 14.99	12.99
Dick Tracy Yellows	Sizes 4-7	Reg. 15.99	13.00

If you carry children's wear, are you signing your sleepwear as flame retardant?

12. How to Promote Your Store with Signing

VERY DAY, STORES AND STORE PERSONNEL do good deeds for their communities. Merchandise is donated. Employees volunteer time. Store executives contribute time and money to local causes. Yet they rarely tell their customers about these services. Why not? Tooting one's horn can be done gracefully in signing.

Another failing of store managers: the belief that "everybody knows that." Ask them, "Where is your return policy sign?" And they reply, "Everybody knows our policy." They forget that over 20% of the United States population moves *every year*. That's a lot of new customers who *don't* know your policies. Keep these reminder signs up every day.

Signs are an opportunity to relate to your customers beyond product benefit and price. How many times has your store done something that excited your employees—but your customers never were told about it? Signs can be little public relations tools. Powerful public relations tools. Think about the possibilities.

Rule #1: When You Do the Right Thing, Tell Everybody

If your store is working on recycling efforts, tell your customers with a sign at every checkout.

JOIN OUR LOCAL RECYCLING PROGRAM

Look for these marks on recyclable plastic

(Print the marks here)

Bring your plastics, glass, and newspapers to:
(list your local recycling stations here)

In 1990, our company recycled

ONE TON of paper

XX POUNDS of aluminum

XX POUNDS of plastic

If your store is supporting a local social, athletic or arts program, sign it at every entrance.

HAPPY HOLIDAYS

from Smith's store.

As a token of our appreciation to you,
we are underwriting the performance of

THE NUTCRACKER

on Saturday, December 15,
at City Hall Center.

BRING IN YOUR CHILD'S OUTGROWN WINTER COAT AND WE'LL GIVE YOU $10.00 OFF A NEW ONE.

We'll donate your old coat to the local
"Keep Kids Warm" program. If you have
other coats, mittens, or hats available
for donation, drop them off at our store
any Monday or Tuesday this month.

Clothing should be in good, clean condition.

SATURDAY IS "TAKE A KID FISHING DAY"

- Fish without a license, if you're fishing with a child

- 25% off all our Snoopy and Starter rods and reels this week only

- FREE 15 minutes of casting instruction with purchase, for children under 12

- $25.00 gift certificate to the youngster 12 or under who brings in the biggest fish in our Kid's Fishing Contest

Registration necessary
Register today at our sporting goods desk

You don't always need ads to make a promotion. Consider how much traffic you get in your store in a week—and think of how many people would see a sign like one of these. You can react to local events in a minute—with a sign.

IF YOUR HOME WAS DAMAGED BY TORNADO

Document the damage!

● Photograph every room, wall, etc.,

● Rent an automatic flash camera or videocam from us.

INQUIRE AT OUR SERVICE DESK

Use customer bulletin boards to talk about more than your advertising. Brag a little. If you don't toot your own horn, who will?

Last Year Smith's

Donated $000.00 to the following organizations:

- **United Way**
- **Cancer Society**
- **Make-A-Wish**
- **Heart Association**
- **Kids Who Care**
- **Muscular Dystrophy**
- **Kidney Foundation**

SMITH'S STORE

and its employees are 100% contributors to

THE UNITED WAY

Can we count on you?

IF YOUR HOME WAS DAMAGED IN LAST WEEK'S FLOOD...

- Rent our clean-up equipment at 50% off.

- For any carpet replacement purchase, take 3 months to pay, no interest charge the first 90 days.

- 30% off all our wallpapers this month. Even custom orders.

Rule #2: Promote Every Service You Offer

Make a list of your services. Then try to locate every place where you tell your customers. Are you depending on salespeople too much? Look for signing opportunities to give your customers another "WE care about you" message.

WE RENT:

★ **Carpet-cleaning equipment**

★ **Heavy-duty floor washer/waxer**

★ **Wallpaper steamer/remover**

Rent by the hour or day. Check our Service Center for prices and to reserve your rental time.

OUR RETURN POLICY:

If you're not happy with it, we want it back.

IF YOU'RE NOT SATISFIED WITH A PURCHASE FROM US, PLEASE BRING IT BACK FOR REFUND OR EXCHANGE.

WE WANT YOU TO BE HAPPY!

FREE DELIVERY

within 15 miles.

Ask about our schedule to your home.

YES

WE DELIVER

FREE ESTIMATES

no matter what size the job.

YES, WE TAKE
MAJOR CREDIT CARDS
Photo I.D.
and telephone number
may be required.

FREE
SEMINARS

Decorating and
do-it-yourself

every

Saturday morning

10:00 a.m.

FREE GIFT BOXES

With any purchase
At our gift stand

Lower Level

LEAVE YOUR PACKAGES WITH US

We'll deliver them to our 8th street door for easy pickup when you've finished shopping.

Just give us 15 minutes!

Money Orders & Postage Stamps

Available at our
Service Counter

Use signing to improve your checklane service—creating an express lane, a "cash only" lane, and don't forget to give instructions on how to speed up the checklanes in general.

EXPRESS CHECKLANE

Ten items or less

CASH ONLY LANE

Rule #3: If You Have One Strong Statement of Policy, Repeat It

As you approach Stew Leonard's store in Norwalk, Connecticut, you will see what looks like a three-ton block of stone. Carved on it is the store's customer service set of rules:

"Rule 1: The customer is always right.

Rule 2: If the customer is ever wrong, re-read rule 1."

Now, you might think that that piece of granite is dramatic enough to get this store's philosophy across, right? Not for Stew Leonard. You will find the rules repeated in the store. Point: if you have an overriding single message, it bears repeating. It bears repeating. It bears repeating.

Rule #4: Attach Your Services to the Appropriate Merchandise

If you're basically a self-service store and you sell merchandise that might give your customer a hernia if he or she lifts it to the shopping cart, offer, in the merchandise sign or near it, whatever you can do to help.

Put your bridal registry signs in the gifts departments. (Pretty basic stuff, but if you don't make the rule, you'll be amazed where those bridal registry signs will appear.) Put your delivery signs by the product too large for the average car. Use common sense. Just get your service signs up. Don't leave your customers alone to figure out what to do. You can lose a sale!

CALL 999

for help to carry this package.

Look for a blue phone.

Bill Blass
Silk Scarves

● Solids, patterns, stripes
● Great gift idea
● FREE gift wrapping

$22.00

Add your services as benefits in product signing. Use checklist signing to give customer service—and also to increase your sales.

CHECK OUR SERVICE CENTER FOR:
- Batteries
- Film
- Returns and refunds
- Post Office
- Cash machine
- Check cashing

CAR WASH CHECKLIST

Sponge	1.49
Plastic bucket	1.99
Soap	2.99
Tar remover (brand)	1.7
Chamois	9.9
Acme wax	3.9
Polish cloth	1.9
TOTAL	23.00

TURKEY BAKING CHECKLIST

Large baking pan	2.39
Rack	1.29
Skewers	.89
Baster	1.49
Aluminum foil (brand)	.78
TOTAL	**$10.00**

You can develop a whole new service specialty business supported entirely by signing. It can be pre-wrapping for Christmas, or custom-made gift packages suited to any time of the year. Notice how much more attractive the gift packages sound when you specify how many are on display. Simply adding the number makes the whole idea sound more appealing and credible.

25 READY-WRAPPED GIFTS ARE ON DISPLAY

$10.00 to $25.00

IN OUR COSMETICS DEPARTMENT

12 CUSTOM-MADE GIFT PACKAGES

are displayed in our fresh produce area

Prices: $15.00 to $50.00

We'll deliver for an extra $5.00

Rule #5: Use Signs to Ask for Customer Feedback

We all like to have people ask us for advice. "What do YOU think?" is a wonderfully complimentary question. Ask your customers what *they* think. Sign your request, and have postage-paid return forms ready for them to take. Ask for ratings on your services. Ask for specific recommendations. Just ask. Encourage customers to tell you what's on THEIR minds. Better YOU know, than 20 of the customer's friends. And then, of course, do something about it!

When I was Vice President of Marketing for a chain in New England, I read every customer feedback message that had to do with sales promotion and advertising. Whenever a customer was really steamed, I made a personal phone call to her or him. They were so pleased to hear from any company—so overwhelmed that I was calling *long distance* to talk to them, that the call itself turned the situation around. When nuts came to bolts, there wasn't much beyond an apology

---

CAN YOU HELP US?

Please tell us what you think about our service and merchandise.

Please take one.

(BOX FOR FORMS)

WE'D LIKE TO HEAR FROM YOU

Please tell us what you like and don't like about our store and services.

Take one.

(BOX FOR FORMS)

necessary. The call turned a complainer into an admirer. If we hadn't had the signing and the forms, I would never have had the opportunity to turn the situation around. Be sure you follow through and capitalize on the potential of customer feedback. In many instances, you will find suggestions that you can implement at low cost, that will make many more customers happy.

You get all this information without the expense of a research project, without the expense of personal interviews in-store, and with the benefit of feedback on an on-going weekly, if not daily, basis. It's fresh research that you can act on quickly. Just with a sign and forms!

Rule #6: Always Sign Upcoming Events and Store Activities

The prime customer for your events is your current customer. Be sure that he or she knows what you are planning. Two weeks isn't too far off to start signing for special appearances and seminars. Always encourage your customers to bring others into the store with them.

LEARN HOW TO WALLPAPER
Expert demonstrations
Saturday, Sept. 15

$5.00 fee includes materials.
Bring a friend. Tickets are 2 for $8.00

KNITTING CLASS

Every Saturday in October, 1-4pm

$2.00 per class

Anyone introducing a beginning knitter will receive a $2.00 gift certificate.

Rule #7: Whenever You Make a Change to the Customer, Sign It

Whether the change is a large inconvenience, such as a remodeling or renovation, or a small change in policy, a simple sign can defuse many customer problems. Simply stating that "we understand it's a problem and we apologize" can do wonders for customers' attitudes. Remember, you are interrupting your customers' normal expectations. Sign. And stay positive.

CAUTION
PROGRESS ZONE

We're renovating to create a better store for you. Sorry for the temporary inconvenience.

PLEASE PARDON OUR DUST

We're renovating to create a better store for you.

Sorry for the temporary inconvenience.

WE WILL CLOSE MONDAY (DATE) FOR INVENTORY

Open Tuesday
9:30am 'til 9:30pm

Weekday hours
9:30am 'til 9:30pm

Sunday hours
12:00pm 'til 6:00pm

WE WILL CLOSE ON
CHRISTMAS EVE AT 4 P.M.

SHOP
9:00 'til 9:00

every day until then!

We will close

THANKSGIVING DAY

Extra shopping hours
Friday and Saturday

Shop 8a.m. 'til 10p.m.

Special service or location signs can be important during rush periods when people who don't normally shop your store may be visiting you. What location-type questions do you get? Try to answer them with signing. A good general service sign is a map of your departments, placed near the front of the store, with a mark and a "You are Here" sign. You might add a list of the top five hard to find items and where they are in your store.

Rule #8: Keep Your "Permanent" Service Signs Looking Good

Many of the signs we've discussed here can be displayed for months if not all year 'round. On your daily trips through the

ALL OUR PIES ARE BAKED IN GLASS OVENWARE PANS AND REQUIRE A $2.00 DEPOSIT.

store, your eyes will begin to glaze over—you simply won't see what's been in front of you day after day. But the customer, who comes in infrequently, will. The customer will notice the Guarantee sign that's dirty and dog-eared.

Discipline yourself and your associates. Plan a regular routine for sign inspections, and have replacements ready for your semi-permanent signs.

Rule #9: Think of Your Signs as Publicity and Public Relations

Many retailers moan that they never get any "free" publicity in their local newspaper. These same retailers overlook the amount of customer traffic they have in their stores every week—and the opportunity that gives them. Whatever your store has done that fits into public relations deserves a sign. Whatever your store is doing that is worthy of publicity is worthy of a sign.

To summarize, when you do the right thing, *tell everybody* that comes into your store, via a sign. *Promote every service* you offer, with a sign. If you have one strong statement of policy, *repeat it* in signs. *Attach* your services to the appropriate merchandise. Use signs to ask for *customer feedback*. Always use signing to announce *upcoming events and store activities*. Always use signing to soften the effect of a change on your customers. Keep all these signs looking good. Make your signs an *integral part* of your public relations and publicity efforts. ◆

13. Measuring Your Sign Program's Cost Effectiveness

ASK A RETAILER ABOUT HIS INVENTORY COSTS, and he'll probably know the number. Ask a retailer about her advertising costs, and she'll probably know the amount. Ask retailers about their signing costs, and they start scratching their heads. Signing costs get buried in supply costs, personnel costs, advertising and "miscellaneous." It is difficult to determine what an individual sign costs but the quest is worth the effort. You may be surprised at what you are paying for a barely satisfactory result.

Many retailers use the wrong people to make signs. If they're relying on hand-written signs, one's best "writer" may also be the higher wage earner. To cost-justify an investment in any sign system, analyze the amount of labor that goes into making signs multiplied by the hourly rate. Any system that can create professional signs *faster* by *more inexpensive labor* can easily be justified.

What this exercise should do is convince you of the payback of an investment in signing—that such an investment can be financially more sound than your everyday investment in advertising!

Part of the equation is "effectiveness." Current research certainly proves effectiveness, as reported in this book's first chapter, "Signs Do Sell—Research Proves It." While research can prove effectiveness in a closely watched and monitored setting, it is more difficult for the individual store owner to monitor and analyze his or her own sales by item. Effectiveness is the more elusive part of the equation, but here are some ways to get perspective.

One way is to isolate ad merchandise sales from non-ad sales. If your advertised merchandise is 15% to 20% of total sales, what is selling the other 80% to 85%? Could signing have an effect on the 80-85%? Count on it!

Sign-making Labor Cost Analysis

Handwritten signs: according to time study experts,[1] handwritten signs each take, on the average, six minutes to make. The very best sign makers can do one every three minutes. That's 20 signs per hour. Computing sign-making labor cost involves dividing the sign-maker's hourly wage by the average number of signs per hour:

If the hourly wage is $8.00 and the signs per hour is 20, then the sign-making labor cost is 40¢ per sign.

This simplified analysis of labor costs alone—not supplies, etc., can come as a surprise to many retailers. What looks cheap many not be inexpensive!

With Insignia's Sign Systems (Impulse and Stylus) as examples, these labor costs can be reduced. By utilizing system features like the memory or QuickPrint function, current users can produce as many as 40 signs per hour (Impulse), up to 100+ per hour (Stylus). That would cut the labor costs by a minimum of 50% to 20¢ per sign, up to as much as 75%+ to 10¢ or less per sign.

An added benefit is that with these systems, current users report that their least skilled employees (often the lower-wage employees) can make signs that are consistent in look and content. An example is a 40,000-square-foot store where the price coordinator was the designated sign maker. She made great signs but could not be available 24 hours a day; and she earned $12.00 per hour. The store now has 6 employees making signs, as necessary, who are paid an average of $6.00 per hour.

[1]Reported by Howard Vork, Manager, Retail Labor Scheduling, SuperValu Stores, Inc. 1990. Minneapolis, MN.

Every successful retailer knows that point-of-purchase signs sell merchandise. But a recent supermarket study has proven that the *look* of those signs has a dramatic impact on their effectiveness. The test, by an internationally-respected market research firm, found that professional-quality signs sold *56% more units* than handwritten signs.

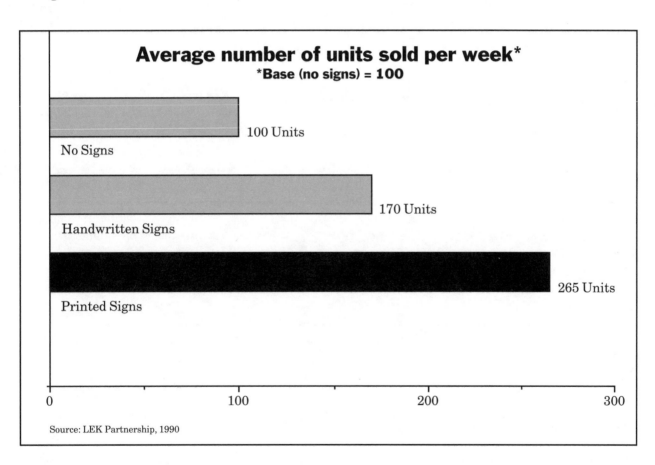

Average number of units sold per week*
*Base (no signs) = 100

No Signs — 100 Units
Handwritten Signs — 170 Units
Printed Signs — 265 Units

0   100   200   300

Source: LEK Partnership, 1990

Now, what would happen to your profits if your signs could be 50% more effective in your store?

RETAIL PRICE	GROSS PROFIT %	GROSS PROFIT $	# OF ITEMS SOLD/WEEK HAND SIGN	# ADD'L ITEMS SOLD/WEEK PRINT SIGN	INCREASED GROSS PROFIT	# ITEMS SIGNED	TOTAL INCREASED GROSS PROFIT
HIGH TURNOVER/LOW MARGIN STORE (e.g., food)							
$1.79	10%	18¢	100	50	$9.00	100	$900.00
MEDIUM TURNOVER/MEDIUM MARGIN (e.g., general merchandise)							
$20.00	20%	$4.00	20	10	$40.00	40	$1,600.00
LOW TURNOVER/HIGH MARGIN (e.g., specialty or jewelry)							
$50.00	40%	$20.00	10	5	$100.00	10	$1,000.00

Let's be more conservative and look at the impact of proper signing on annual sales for three segments of another retail industry:

These approaches are examples from clients of Insignia Systems and are intended to be a guide to help you forecast your own store sales and profit figures.

	HARDWARE	HOME CTR	DYI LMBR
Average Sales Volume	$776,600	$3,750,500	$2,776,200
Average Transaction	$11.18	$25.60	$58.14
# Customer Transactions	69,463	146,504	47,750
If signing would add $1 of additional sales for every four transactions, the increased sales volume would be:	$17,365	$36,626	$11,937
Average Gross Margin	35.9%	26.9%	24.9%
Gross Margin Dollar Increase	$6,234	$9,852	$2,972

So let's get back to cost. Professional sign making systems will vary in cost depending on design, graphic and overall system capabilities. With sign systems, as in most cases, you get what you pay for. For the purposes of this example, let's say that a professional sign making system and a one year supply of cardstock would cost around $3,000. Subtract from that what your current program is costing you in supplies. Assume that you won't be adding any people or subtracting any people, at least for this exercise.

You have choices in how you account for the sign-making equipment. It may be leased and considered a straight expense or it may be capitalized and depreciated. For this exercise, let's look at the charts below.

> *You may be surprised at what you are paying for a barely satisfactory result.*

There is another way to look at cost-effectiveness. Understanding that a sign *does* increase sales, ask yourself the following questions. Assign a dollar value to each of the following improvements to your business. The dollar value could reflect increased sales, recovery of lost sales today due to no signs, or just a dollar value for efficiency. What would you pay per month if these improvements actually happened?

$2,500.00 for equipment
+500.00 for supplies
—————
$3,000.00 total expense

$3,000.00 total expense
—   less cost of
        current program
—————
=   incremental cost
        or savings of new
        sign program

$500.00 first year capital
        investment
+500.00 for supplies
—————
$1,000.00 first year expense

$1,000.00 first year expense
        less cost of
        current program
—————
=   incremental cost
        or savings of new
        sign program

What Would You Pay per Month for These Improvements?

1. Signs when you need them.
Have you ever wanted to change a price
but couldn't?
A special sign but knew it would take too long? .... $ _____ /month

2. Consistent look.
No sloppy printing.
A better image of quality for your store .... $ _____ /month

3. Feature/benefits on signs.
"Silent salespeople"
and the increased sales you're bound to get .... $ _____ /month

4. More sign control.
Do you use vendor signs even though you don't want to?
Have you always received signs exactly the way you wanted them?
Ever wanted to be able to react instantly to local conditions? .... $ _____ /month

5. Professional image.
Printed signs with feature/benefits are a must for a professional look .... $ _____ /month

6. Increased store sales.
(Check your figures from the cost-effectiveness charts above) .... $ _____ /month

7. Increased store profits.
You'll be able to direct customers
to your better-margin goods, private labels, etc. .... $ _____ /month

8. Increased employee motivation.
Everyone feels better
when the store environment looks professional .... $ _____ /month

TOTAL PER MONTH .... $ _____

TOTAL PER YEAR .... $ _____

Less cost of equipment .... — $ _____

POTENTIAL INCREASE IN VALUE .... $ _____

On average, low-cost sign-printing equipment will pay for itself within one year—an unusually fast return on investment. To make a comparison to advertising—take the same $3,000 and invest it in advertising:

$ _____ Total ad merchandise sold

— _____ Cost of goods sold

= $ _____ Incremental gross margin

— _____ Cost of ad

= $ _____ (Profit or loss on ad)

Even if you add a small amount of incremental non-ad sales the incremental gross margin rarely equals your advertising investment!

> ## On average, low-cost sign equipment will pay for itself within a year.

If you take your daily sales figures and establish a base sales figure for your regular-priced merchandise, you can estimate what increase you had in nonadvertised merchandise during the sale period:

$ _____ Total value of extra non-ad merchandise sold

— $ _____ Cost of goods for these items

= $ _____ Incremental gross margin

Adding up the total gross margin for your incremental *ad sales* and your incremental *non-ad sales* will still be a disappointment. Does this mean that you shouldn't advertise?

Of course not. Advertising has many purposes, including bringing new customers into your store and retaining current customers. There are benefits to advertising that cannot be measured in dollars and cents—just as there are benefits to *signing* that can't be measured in dollars and cents. Both, for instance, have a "carryover" effect in the customers' minds. Both affect your customers' perception of your store relative to competition and each customer's value/price equation.

What this exercise should do is convince you of the payback of an investment in signing—that such an investment can be financially more sound than your everyday investment in advertising! The potential payback is well worth your attention. ◆

14. How Many Signs Do You Need?

THE NUMBER OF SIGNS YOU NEED IS IN DIRECT PROPORTION to the price image you want for your retail operation. It's that simple. If you have handwritten signs, they will always look like too many. If you have neat, printed signs, you can sign much more product and still look like a quality operation.

You can add a significant amount of signing to gondolas and runs by using shelf-talkers—the 3 1/2" x 5 1/2" size signs that, if printed, can give lots of benefit copy as well as price. A rule of thumb for these signs is one sign every 3 to 4 feet of gondola *shelf*.

Supermarkets and other high-volume retailers often put their prices, values and product information on scannable bar-coded shelf tags. Shelf tags are necessary to price every item, but often lack the visual impact necessary to really "sell" merchandise. These tags will become a more effective selling tool as graphics become easier to incorporate into them, but signs will out- perform them every time. To see how signs will affect sales, try this: take any 12-foot section that has barcoded shelf tags and make a small 3 1/2" x 5 1/2" sign on any one item—even the highest-priced item—and watch what happens.

Every endcap should have a feature display and a 5 1/2 x 7″ sign (at least) announcing your offering. The merchandise doesn't have to be promotionally priced—review the chapter on research to see how such a presentation can increase sales on a very ordinary product.

If you are a fashion-forward store, you need a few signs to tell people about the latest trends. You need a few signs to indicate mark-downs and clearance merchandise. As a general rule, the higher the margins, the higher the prices, the fewer signs you need.

If you are a price/value dis-

The more "commodity" the business, the more emphasis on price and hence, more signing.

counter, you need to evaluate each area of your store, to balance price and value or quality. For instance, if you have apparel, you might want to emphasize trend signing, then work on a mix of trend signs and price signs in order to give your apparel areas a good mix of what the customer wants: trends and price. This demands store tours and a good many judgment calls.

One of the rules of the trade is that the more "commodity" the business, the more emphasis on price and hence, more signing. There isn't much difference between one store's Health and Beauty items and another store's. Everything is

similar: both brands and prices. The general rule here is, he who signs the most gives the most signals to the customer of price. Naturally, if your prices are out of line, the customers will discover that and quit visiting your store. I am talking about a situation where your prices are basically on a par with competition.

You will notice that when we have discussed price we have added "value" to it. That's because "value" is extremely important in the signing message. Just as handwritten signs indicate "price," they don't indicate "value." And today's customers want value. So it is important to wrap each product in some semblance of value. That means *not too many signs*. Once sign overload has occurred, you have lost your "value" image.

Let's get back to the idea of commodity versus unique. The more commodities you sell, the harder you have to pound price. There is no other differentiating selling idea. And the more you have to watch your competition regarding their prices and promotions. Once you have a unique or new product, you can price discreetly and probably not even sign the price. Just announce that you have the product.

To help you approach your own business, please refer to the chart on the next page, which describes signing according to three general merchandise areas—commodities, basics and new trends. Each one is handled differently.

Another way to analyze your merchandise and its best signing is to study the progress of any one item from introduction to clearance. Each piece of its development can require a different signing philosophy. Look at the bell curve illustration (next page) to estimate the amount of sales any one retailer can expect on any one product. First, it's in a testing mode. You buy a few and "test" customer demand.

Testing: sign the trend. Add benefits to overcome resistance to newness. Basically very few signs, and price is not most important.

Rapid growth period: sign the trend and everyday price. There's much more merchandise being presented, thus more signs are needed, featuring benefits before price.

Pre-peak: sales are increasing but not as rapidly. About the same number of signs, more emphasis on price.

Peak: sales have leveled. Watch for decline. Merchandise will be heavily promoted during major sale events, or to create a major traffic draw.

Early decline: fashion forward stores will be starting to clear this merchandise. Watch your price points.

Highly promotional period: price has become most important and should be featured every day, with frequent off-price promotions.

Clearance: all price oriented. Percent off or magic price points.

There are many judgment calls to be made in your store. The following charts are here to help you and your associates work out what is best in your very individual case. Please refer to Chapter 15 "Organizing an Effective Sign Program" for more information. ◆

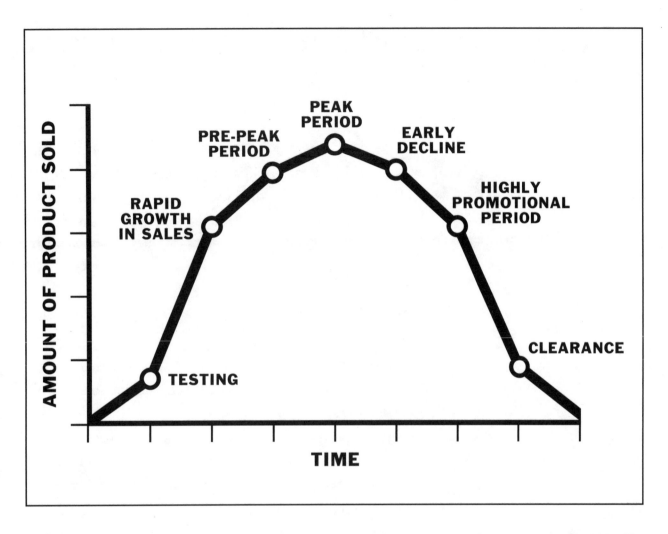

MERCHANDISE	PRICING	SIGN CONTENT	AMOUNT OF SIGNS
Commodities	Very competitive	Price plus benefits	Heavy
Basics	Moderately competitive	Benefits plus price	Moderate 1 per 4′ shelf
New trends	Not a #1 issue	Trend name	Light

15. Organizing an Effective Signing Program

BECAUSE THE SIGN-MAKING PROCESS crosses several areas in a retail organization, it is easy to lose direction and—most important—discipline. Each buyer has a different attitude about signs. Each department head has a different attitude about signs. The result can make a significant difference in sales between stores—and between departments.

We have established the selling capabilities of good signs. Now the question is, how do you make good signs happen? There is no simple solution. It's a process. It's an ongoing program that takes cooperation from all areas of your business.

If you have a large operation, it takes cooperation from practically all your headquarters departments: buyers, merchandisers, stores, advertising and signing. If you have a small organization, the group is smaller, but the discussion and questions remain the same: what is your store's current image and what is the purpose of each department in your store? What is your store's *desired* image? In total and department by department? When you have answers to these few basic questions, the group can focus on how to make each department—and the total store—more effective. More customer friendly. More service oriented. More fun.

#1: Does Your Sign Program Reflect Your Store and its Merchandise?

The basic questions are: what is the mission of each selling area? And does the current presentation look like that mission to the customers? An "assortment/quality" presentation demands fewer signs, with benefits rather than price signing. A "value/price" image demands significantly more signs. Trend signs should indicate new merchandise and new fashion ideas. A simple organizing process is to use group tours of a store, getting consensus on what your business should look like. It is important that everyone involved in signing be part of the tours. Everyone needs to believe that they have ownership of the program—or the disciplines won't stay in place. You need a committee representing buyers, stores, signing—and customers.

In my experience, store managers are too shy about asking customers for advice and information. Several organizations I have worked with have had customer "councils" which become a sounding

In my experience, store managers are too shy about asking customers for advice and information.

board for proposed changes and current policies as well as merchandise.

In one case, we gave members of our group a shopping list and asked them to find the products in the store. We tracked them to see where they went first, looking for merchandise that could logically be in several possible locations. It helped us plan the store to be more customer friendly.

In another case, we took individual departments and asked our group to rank them against significant competition. We asked the advisory board members to fill out a simple form which ranked us according to various strengths: prices, assortments, quality, etc. We

discovered that their concept of our competition was not what we had assumed. They told us that we had competition in other fields of retailing which we were ignoring. Hearing from your customers isn't always pleasant, but it is a learning experience!

Before you implement any major sign campaign, take it to a customer panel—a focus group—to hear what the campaign means to "real people." Have the group tour your store and see the signs in action, then give you a second opinion. It will surprise you. It may save you money. It will confirm your faith in signing—and in the intelligence of the general public. People are very sophisticated about claims, about advertising and about value.

#2: Is Your Basic Store Presentation Well Organized?

Before you can sign, you need to decide *where* your merchandise, in general, will be placed on the selling floor. Presentation comes before signs. Again, while each department may have some variations, a general philosophy of presentation needs to be agreed upon for the total store.

A general rule of in-store presentation organization is shown below.

This rough plan could direct the merchandise on an individual gondola in your hardware department, or be the organization guide for your total ready-to-wear area. The up-front presentation of change on a regular basis gives the customer the news first, and uses clearance to draw your customer through the basic merchandise.

By giving space (endcaps,

HARDLINES EXAMPLE FLOOR PLAN

WALL OR INSIDE AISLE

NON-SEASONAL BASICS
Sign with customer benefits

CLEARANCE MERCHANDISE
Sign according to percentage off

NON-SEASONAL BASICS
Sign with customer benefits

BASICS

NEW TRENDS
Sign to label trends and introduce newness

SEASONAL MERCHANDISE
Sign major price points and merchandise groups—emphasize customer benefits

SEASONAL

SEASONAL BASICS
Sign major price points and merchandise groups—emphasize customer benefits

SEASONAL INTRODUCTIONS
Emphasize benefits to overcome reaction to newness

MAIN AISLE

MAIN AISLE

main aisle displays, etc.) to new merchandise up front, you look like your stock is changing much more rapidly than it really is. You look more exciting. Use this basic layout as a start-ing point for discussion about each area of your business.

There are situations where you would want to dramatically change these examples. If you are a specialty store in a mall, you might reverse the order of the merchandise. Clearance racks might be practically out-side your door, to attract mall walkers and get people to stop at your entrance. Next, you

SOFTLINES EXAMPLE FLOOR PLAN

WALL

WALL

CLEARANCE
Sign according to
percentage off

BASICS
Sign major price points
and merchandise groups—emphasize
customer benefits

NON-SEASONAL BASICS
Sign with
customer benefits

FIRST MARKDOWNS
Sign with
customer benefits

SEASONAL BASICS
Sign major price
points and
merchandise
groups—emphasize
customer benefits

SEASONAL BASICS
Sign major price
points and
merchandise
groups—emphasize
customer benefits

NEW TREND
Sign to label trends and
introduce newness

NEW TREND
Sign to label trends and
introduce newness

MAIN AISLE

MAIN AISLE

might present a mix of first markdowns and basics, with new trends displayed on the side and rear walls. It might differ with the seasons. The point is to get philosophical agreement on presentation formats.

Next, you need to agree on a range of details. How many signs per foot can one gondola handle? How many signs per endcap before the customer gets confused? If common sense dictates one sign per apparel fixture, does every fixture need a sign, or should it be a general rule: every fourth fixture on an everyday basis, with exceptions for major sales? You, your buyers and store managers need to agree on the rules. Consensus here will help discipline later.

#3: Have You Planned Every Sign Location?

Take out a floor plan of your store. Plot the signing per department, and check again. Then take inventory of your sign holders. Do you have enough holders, of the right size

You can sign a significant number of products without interfering with the customer's ability to pull the item off the shelf.

and attachment, to present the signing you want? What will it cost to accomplish the right signing? This exercise can save you money, since you will know exactly what the requirements will be. No odd signholders languishing in the stockrooms! When you are confident of the sign-holding situation, make the signs necessary to fulfill your mission. Get them up in a store, and repeat your tour. Is the actual result what you, as a group, envisioned? What do customers think? What do the store personnel think?

Make adjustments, and set your standards. You should have general agreement about how many signs, where, and on what.

On your long runs and gondolas, don't overlook the possibilities of hardworking 3½″ x 5½″ shelf-talkers. When they are uniformly printed with price and benefit information, they can increase sales and customer service. Assuming that you organize your product vertically, you can sign a significant number of products without interfering with the customers' ability to pull the item off the shelf.

#4: Are You Currently Using Handwritten Signs?

To my knowledge, every retailer who has printed sign capabilities, with the possible exception of the food industry, also has a rule about handwritten signs: NEVER ALLOW THEM. That rule is an eloquent condemnation of handwritten signs! Yes, hand-made signs are quick, inexpensive and can be done by almost anybody. But they are often hard to read and they lack effectiveness. There is simply no space or ability to add the customer benefits that can increase sales.

The technology exists today that successfully bridges the needs of small store operations that want fast, low-cost signs—and the desire for the professional quality look of printed signs. I know of one grocery store operation (with five stores in the Midwest) which has, in one store alone, 16 people capable of making printed signs, successfully and happily, on a machine that is as easy as a typewriter to use. It can be done. Inexpensively, too.

If you still think that handwritten signs are desirable in your store, please refer again to the chapter on research. Today's customers are our most sophisticated. They own computers, word-processors and home offices. They work in high-tech environments. They are busy, time-stressed and in need of information as well as some ambiance. They appreciate printed signs!

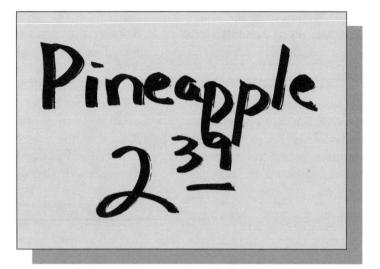

#5: What's Best for You: Centralized or Decentralized Signing?

Once a retail organization has grown from one location to several, it has to face the issue of centralized services. Centralization offers control, efficiency and standardization. But at some point in the proliferation of stores, centralization can offer inflexibility, inability to respond to local conditions, and questionable efficiency.

Today's technology allows a retail chain to create a sign-making hybrid—with headquarters' production of all chain-wide sale signing, planogram signs, trend signs, etc. Individual stores can create matching signs to tie into local events, correct a price or change a price to react to competition. Here you have all the efficiencies of centralized sign-making with the immediacy of decentralized. It can be done.

CENTRALIZED SIGNING

PROS

1. Efficiency—sign is created once for all stores
Copies of master sign are inexpensive to produce

2. Quality control of copy claims and layout —consistent look

3. Central location, close to buyers and merchandisers—easier communication and direction—especially of sales

4. Individual stores are assured of having a "corporate" look

5. General "clearance" and "sale" signs and prices can be used to cover local conditions

CONS

1. Some inefficiency—not all stores may need every sign
Copies of all signs can be expensive to mail to all stores, especially air express service

2. Inability to react to local opportunities, conditions

3. Distance from stores and the "front lines"
If stores differ in format or content, opportunities can be missed

4. Inflexibility. Difficult to adjust quickly to local competition

5. If there is a merchandise glitch or any individual store variation in format, you'll have problems

6. Corporate look can be sterile looking and lack local friendliness

7. Speed—getting special signs, replacing wrong signs, etc., can take precious days if not weeks

8. Price-only signs lack product benefits and aren't as effective as they could be

#6: Do You Have a Policy Regarding Vendor Signs?

Many retailers fall into the trap of putting up only the signs that are provided for them by the vendor or cooperative. There are reasons for this:

- The signs are professionally printed.
- The signs tie in with national or coop advertising.
- It's so easy.

It is important to use signing as a total merchandising tool, not just as an extension of the manufacturers' or cooperatives' sales efforts. Maintaining control over the store is an important rule for all retailers. Don't let manufacturers or wholesalers take over your store!

In large chain operations a vendor has to go through hoops to get its signing in stores. Large chains have their own image to protect. They have strict guidelines as to what kind of signing can be in store, and where. They have presentation experts on staff with different priorities than the manufacturer; they will want *their* presentation customized. They have legitimate concerns which the smaller stores should consider. For instance, the manufacturer's signing will undoubtedly focus on the manufacturer's logo—not on customer benefits. Manufacturers' signing may be too large for your presentation—overwhelming your whole department. Your presentation will look identical to your competition's.

It is one thing to consider a manufacturer's endcap presentation and method of organizing the product if you are planning to achieve easier selling or more sales per square foot. It is another thing to consider the manufacturer's signing.

You need to have a consistent look in your store. Manufacturers' signing destroys consistency. You need a value/price presentation—manufacturers' signing rarely has space for price identification.

Any retailer has to walk a fine line between the desire to promote brand names—and the problem of being overwhelmed by a manufacturer's logo . . .

DECENTRALIZED SIGNING	
PROS	**CONS**
1. Immediate response to individual store needs: merchandise or prices	1. The production of a large percentage of signs will be duplicated effort in all stores
2. Ability to localize communication	2. Product benefits may not be as strong or clear as headquarter copy May vary from store to store
3. No mailing costs from headquarters to stores	3. Signs may not tie into headquarter's plans regarding sales, promotions, merchandise
4. Product benefits can be localized	
5. People closest to customer are making signs	

between the desire to focus on customer benefits—and the manufacturer's reasons for its signing. It is rare to have both manufacturer and retailer focusing on the same strategy. Don't be a pushover for the manufacturers' reps. Think it over. Ask how you could do it better.

#7: Have You Planned the Routine of Sign-Making Itself?

Who is responsible for making sure that the signing program is carried out—day in and day out? In a large centralized operation, it could be organized like this:

Buyer
- Knows when new merchandise will hit the stores and when price breaks will occur (markdowns, advertising, etc.)
- Organizes the correct information about merchandise, and about pricing.
- Sets priorities for merchandise signing.
- Gives information to sign shop
- Plans major sets of new merchandise, seasonal changes

Sign Production
- Writes sign copy per information from buyer
- Distributes signs to proper stores
- Gives information to stores regarding priorities
- Checks stores and floor layouts for correct amount of signs
- Reminds buyers on a routine basis, inquiring about:
  - new merchandise trends
  - out-of-date signs that should come down
  - major seasonal sets of new merchandise
  - customer benefit

Store Manager Assistant or Area Manager
- Checks in signs and makes sure they are up
- Checks for out-of-date signs still up. Alerts sign shop of problems.
- Trains department heads, group managers to look for sign problems, requests signs as he or she sees needs
- Executes major seasonal sets of new merchandise
- Decides sign and merchandise presentation changes needed on a daily, weekly basis, depending on sellout's, merchandise changes, etc.

That is a lot of activity but it is necessary in order to maximize the selling potential of your signing. If you are a manager of a single store, you can't possibly manage and do all of the above yourself. Delegate the activities; organize your people and organize a review process so that the time spent is efficient and productive. Make signing a routine part of your activities, and it *will* get done and done right. Whether you are large or small, the key is a sign system that everyone can use, and that allows fast production turnaround. It's those last-minute changes that cause signing glitches—and then no sign at all!

#8: Do You Review Your Signing Regularly?

Whenever management executives visit a store, or whenever a manager reviews a department, signing should be a vital part of the discussion. Here is an excellent opportunity to study what is really happening versus what was planned. To facilitate what can become a long laundry list of details, here is a suggested Store Tour Checklist for presentation and signing issues.

STORE TOUR CHECKLIST

ACTIVITY	GOOD IDEAS	PROBLEMS

1. Review this week's sale signing
   - Are all advertised items signed? (list)
   - Do any ad items have traditional problems, such as always needing *two* signs for back-to-back signing, etc.
   - Are all advertised items easy to locate or are there problems with customers confusing sale merchandise with adjacent non-sale merchandise?

2. Review general signing policies
   - Are there any out-of-date signs still up?
   - Are there enough signs, per agreement, per fixture, gondola, etc.?
   - Are there too many signs in any area? Too few?

3. Review general sign quality issues
   - Are signs consistent—legible and neat?
   - Are the benefits well presented?
   - Do the signs, in general, enhance the appearance of your store?

4. Review trend signing
   - Is what's new proudly out in front for the customers to see, and is it properly signed?
   - Are any trends missing signs?
   - Does the customer understand the trend?

5. Review any problems surfaced by store managers and associates

6. Communicate this checklist to buyers and sign personnel

7. Check sign department and stores to make sure proper signing has been prepared and sent

#9: Do You Have an Annual, Major Review of Your Signing Program?

Let's assume you are planning to organize a group of your associates, (and ideally some customers) to study your signing requirements and implement changes and improvements in your signing program. To help you facilitate the process, the next page offers a simple worksheet. You can present the worksheet at your first meeting, so the group can negotiate deadlines and volunteer for responsibilities. Ask the group for suggestions as to additional steps that should be added to your process, according to your particular business needs.

On-going review (repeat this process annually). ◆

SIGNING WORKSHEET

ACTIVITY	WHO IS RESPONSIBLE?	DATE	SUPPORT
❏ If possible, send photographer and sign person to store; photograph presentations and signs			
❏ Meet to review slides and discuss signing General guidelines			
• Number of signs per department			
• Sign problems			
• Who is captain of this effort?			
• Which store is test site?			
• When is best date for visit?			
❏ Store visit			
• Where is good signing?			
• How did it happen?			
• Review guidelines vs. "real world"			
• Check number of signs			
• Check number of signs per area			
• Get feedback from store personnel			
❏ Report on consensus			
• Good signing to stay			
• Signing needed per guideline			
• Request for sign copy			
❏ Signholder inventory—what is in stores vs. new needs			
❏ Evaluate sign system			
• Centralized vs. decentralized, use of hybrid system			
❏ Order signs and signholders			
❏ Set up store			
❏ Store visit			
❏ Revisions list/action			
❏ Order revised signs, etc.			
❏ Feed information, signs to other stores			
❏ Store visit to review signs during major sale			
❏ Staff meeting to discuss			
❏ Store visit to review signs after new merchandise set			
❏ Staff meeting to discuss			
❏ On-going review (repeat this process annually.)			

16. Before You Buy Sign-Making Equipment–Considerations and Comparisons

MOST RETAILERS' SIGN-MAKING SYSTEMS are fraught with frustration. There isn't any question that signs help retailers sell more merchandise. I have yet to have a retailer, of any size, tell me that signs do *not* do the job. They are not unhappy with *signs*, they are unhappy with the *process*. They want more signs! They want more flexibility in sign-making. They want faster turn-around. Getting the signs made is a hassle—and a long-term hassle can make everyone involved decide that "it's just not worth it."

A book on signage wouldn't be complete unless it addressed the basic sign-making problem: getting signs made quickly and professionally. Which of the many sign systems will do the best job for you? I have seen almost every system available. I've participated in the purchase of a few over the years. I have had departments of people searching for sign-making solutions. I think I understand the advantages of many and the disadvantages of all.

I will assume that you have undergone a thorough analysis of your own store's needs. You have followed the directions and checklists in Chapter 17, "Organizing an Effective Signing Program." You understand exactly your retail business needs. You have worked out the centralized/decentralized issues, and have cost projections for your current program. Now I assume that you are looking at a new sign system. To help you evaluate the many products available, here is another trusty checklist.

Questions for the Sign-Making Equipment Vendor

❑ 1. Does the system make professionally printed signs? (Any product that uses guides for hand lettering, for example, is not worth the money.)

❑ 2. Does it print in different typestyles? You will want a consistent look throughout your store, but different typestyles can add interest.

❑ 3. Will its design capabilities allow a customized look for your store? (You don't want to look like the competition!)

❑ 4. Is it user-friendly? Most aren't. If you can't make a sign in minutes or even seconds, chances are you will not use it as often as you should. Being user-friendly is extremely important!

❑ 5. Can you try the product in your store? This will be the ultimate test of whether your people can really make a sign.

❑ 6. Is there a guarantee? Will the manufacturer stand behind the product if it doesn't work up to your expectations?

❑ 7. Does it use sign card stock? The minimum thickness should be 7.5 mil, about the thickness of a postcard. Paper signs aren't sturdy enough to maintain a professional look.

❑ 8. Does it make at least 11 x 14″ signs and smaller? (It would be better if it made 22 x 28″ as well, but 95% of your signs will likely be 11 x 14″ and smaller.)

❑ 9. Does the manufacturer have a toll-free number for support and questions?

❑ 10. What kind of training is provided, for how long and at what cost? I have seen systems which require at least 100 hours to learn. You then have a dedicated operator specialist. Is that what you want? Make sure you are pre-pared for introductory training time and retraining in case you have people turnover.

❑ 11. Can the system be located in the store, and even used by departments? Only the largest chains can use centralized systems. (I am convinced that the ability to create signs at the store level gives a retailer maximum flexibility, adaptability and opportunity.)

❑ 12. If you need signs on a weekend or at night, can just about anyone in the store make a sign? This is the real world. You don't want to be caught with a wrong price or wrong information on a sign.

❑ 13. Can you get color on the sign? Colorful sign card stock is a big plus. Can you get your logo on the sign if you want it?

❑ 14. Is the system affordable? I am confident that a sign-making system *that is used* will justify its investment. Good signs are free—they are effective enough to offset a reasonable extra cost.

Questions to Ask Your Own Organization

❏ 1. Does the system under consideration fulfill the *most pressing wants* of your associates regarding signing?

❏ 2. Are you and your associates in agreement regarding who should be allowed to create signs?

❏ 3. Who will be the champion of the new system, making sure that it is introduced positively to the store employees and everyone involved?

❏ 4. Who will make all the signing decisions of your store, regarding formats, customizing, colors, pre-printed headlines?

❏ 5. A new sign system can trigger an organizational change. Therefore, how will this affect your organization chart? Will there be more sign-making people? Dedicated sign-making operators? Or a smaller sign department? Does anyone need to be reassigned?

❏ 6. Who has charge of the signing budget and how will he or she control it?

❏ 7. Who will negotiate with the sign-making supplier, and sign the contract?

❏ 8. Do you have clear guidelines for the people who will be making signs?

❏ 9. What is a reasonable price for sign equipment that fits your needs? (Don't waste your time and vendors' time considering equipment that is beyond your budget.)

❏ 10. Do you buy or lease? A cost analysis of each might tell you that one is much better (for YOU) than the other. ◆

About the Author

SONJA LARSEN has had 30 years of advertising experience, ranging from copywriting at Campbell-Mithun Advertising (at that time, the largest ad agency in the Midwest, outside of Chicago) to being Senior Vice President of Target Stores. When she began her career at Target in 1978, the chain had fewer than 60 stores. By the time she retired to start her own business in 1988, Target had 360 stores.

At Target, all signing for every store was centralized—and the department reported to Ms. Larsen. The chain's phenomenal growth demanded an equally phenomenal effort to organize and deliver a constantly more sophisticated sign package to more and more stores. Proof of the successful efforts of her associates in the sign department is in how many other discount stores' executives have visited Target and "knocked off" its signing innovations.

Ms. Larsen's formal title for most of her tenure at Target was Senior Vice President of Advertising, Sales Promotion and Merchandise Presentation. Thus, planogramming, hardlines and softlines merchandise presentation also reported to her.

Before her career at Target, Ms. Larsen was Vice President of Marketing for a chain of junior department stores in New England; Vice President of Advertising for two department store chains, and advertising director of Dayton's department stores. In each location, her department's work was recognized with national advertising awards.

She is a popular speaker and presenter—she has worked with the Radio Advertising Bureau in its training seminars and is published in RAB's manual on vendor cooperation in advertising. She has worked with the Newspaper Advertising Bureau and chaired an advisory committee for the Audit Bureau of Circulation.

As a consultant, she has led strategic planning retreats for

Sonja Larsen

The Guthrie Theater management and artistic staff, Twin Cities Public Television management and many others. Just to illustrate her diversity: her client list has included a regional chain of lumber and do-it-yourself stores, manufacturers, inventors, newspapers and radio stations, chambers of commerce, automotive after-market retailers, a hospital and even a group of consulting psychologists.

Her diverse background enables her to adjust her vision from small-store operations to large chains—from small clients struggling to break even to successful multi-billion-dollar operations.

A high point in her career came in 1987 when she was recognized nationally at the Retail Advertising Conference, named Ad Person of the Year and elected to RAC's Hall of Fame. She was the second discount advertiser so recognized in the Hall of Fame's 30-year history.

Today, she is president of her own consulting company, Fawn Creek, Inc., located in the serene and beautifully scenic Brainerd Lakes area in northern Minnesota. She is a regular columnist for the Retail Advertising and Marketing Newsletter; she is a member of RAC's board of directors, and is on the board of directors for two advertising agencies. She occasionally writes articles for *Home Based and Small Business Network* magazine.

Her previous board work includes: Minneapolis Arts Commission, Minneapolis Downtown YMCA, Working Opportunities for Women and Minneapolis Red Cross.

Besides her interests in marketing and management, she and her husband are avid fishermen and are active in conservation efforts. She is a Trustee for the Minnesota Chapter of The Nature Conservancy and on the Board of Directors for Brainerd's Paul Bunyan Conservation Arboretum.

With her writing, marketing and management background, she has the unique combination of qualities to discuss a subject that has not been given sufficient attention: the subject of successful merchandise signing. ◆

99 Questions and Thought-starters for Small Retail Operations

In General

❏ 1. How many forms of advertising do you have? Print? Broadcast? In-store?

❏ 2. Do you consider merchandise signing to be an important part of your sales promotion efforts?

❏ 3. Do you regularly walk your store?

❏ 4. Are you stopping the customer with your signs?

❏ 5. Can you talk to every customer who comes into your store?

❏ 6. Could you increase the "ring" if you could keep people in your store longer?

❏ 7. Are you aware of the fact that 60 to 70% of the buying decisions (which brand, etc.,) are made in the store?

❏ 8. Do you spend more on outside advertising than you do on in-store merchandising and signing?

❏ 9. Are you ever embarrassed by your own signs?

❏ 10. Do people come to your store and walk out without buying anything?

❏ 11. What targets have you set for sales goals this year?

❏ 12. How are you going about achieving those goals?

❏ 13. Are merchandise signs part of your program?

❏ 14. How's business? Could it be better?

❏ 15. If you could get 25¢ more in sales from every customer (or $1.00 more from every fourth customer), what would it mean in plus sales? Gross margin?

Competition

❏ 16. How does your competition do their signing?

❏ 17. Do you feel that felt-tip-pen-made signs just don't stand up to competition?

❏ 18. How do you compare with your competition as far as customer service is concerned? Would feature/benefit signs help you in this area?

❏ 19. Do you regularly walk your competitors' stores?

❏ 20. Have you ever wondered, "How can I compete with the big operators?"

❏ 21. If you can't advertise as much as they can—can you sign as well? Or better?

Sign Production

❏ 22. What size signs do you normally use?

❏ 23. Do you do your signing any differently today than when you started your business?

❏ 24. If you had a fast, professional in-house sign-making system that you could use immediately, what would it be worth to you?

❏ 25. Would more control over sign production be of value?

❏ 26. What type of merchandise signs do you produce now?

❏ 27. Have you considered changing your method of sign production?

❏ 28. Would you do more signs if the process were easier and quicker?

❏ 29. If you have updated your store, what have you done to improve the effectiveness of your signing program?

❏ 30. Are you confident that your current signing is producing the sales you would like?

❏ 31. Does more than one person in your store make your signs?

❏ 32. Do you just make price-only signs?

❏ 33. Are the only signs you use the ones provided by a vendor or co-op?

❏ 34. Why do you think your co-op or franchise sends you the signs that they do?

❏ 35. Do you like making signs?

❏ 36. Would you change your signs more often if they were easier to make?

❏ 37. What do you think of when the word "signs" is mentioned? Hand done? Sloppy? Not enough information? No price comparison?

❏ 38. Are you still using one of those Gutenberg-type printing presses in your point of sale signing?

❏ 39. Who does your merchandise signing? How long does it take?

❏ 40. Exactly how much time is being spent now on merchandise signing in your store?

❏ 41. How much does your current program actually cost?

Sign Content

❏ 42. Are you aware that a price-only sign on non-sale merchandise can actually decrease sales?

❏ 43. Do your signs routinely contain features/benefits as well as price?

❏ 44. Do you think of shelf-talker signs as the last, pre-purchase communications link between you and your customer?

❏ 45. Do you believe that signs can be "silent salespeople?" Are *your* signs?

❏ 46. Are your signs effectively communicating as "silent salespeople"?

❏ 47. Do you tie local events and happenings into your signing program?

❏ 48. Are you stopping the customer with your signs?

❏ 49. Do you think product-benefit signing could improve customer relations and how people feel about your store?

Merchandising

❏ 50. How do you merchandise your carry-over or overstocked items?

❏ 51. How do you sign your overstock?

❏ 52. Do you ever find that new inventory sits in a back room waiting for a sign?

❏ 53. Would you like to increase your store's sales without increasing floor space?

❏ 54. Have you looked into merchandising programs from outside resources?

❏ 55. What merchandising tools do you have now that can help you?

❑ 56. Did you ever have an idea for an in-store promotion that you didn't implement because you couldn't do an effective sign?

❑ 57. Is in-store merchandising and signing often overlooked because it just takes too long to get what you want?

❑ 58. Are your shelves properly stocked?

❑ 59. Do sale items monopolize your shelf space?

❑ 60. Do off-price sales monopolize your time and attention?

❑ 61. Do you sign all your closeouts, overstocks, sale, new, seasonal and impulse items?

❑ 62. How do you plan your displays of seasonal items to maximize their sales?

❑ 63. Do you cross-merchandise your sale merchandise with regular-priced stock that is related?

❑ 64. How are you pursuing higher-margin sales right now?

❑ 65. Is higher-ticket merchandise getting the same attention as sale merchandise?

❑ 66. Is higher-margin merchandise adequately signed to sell?

*Sometimes writing things down helps you find the way **into**, not out of, a problem. Therein lies the solution.*

❑ 67. Is your merchandise turnover satisfactory? Could it be better?

❑ 68. Are your customers reacting to merchandise you've signed?

❑ 69. Do you feel that people buy only because of price?

❑ 70. What targets have you set for sales goals this year?

❑ 71. How are you going about achieving those goals?

❑ 72. Is feature/benefit signing a high priority in your merchandising program?

Cross-merchandising

❑ 73. Is cross-merchandising being used effectively in your store today?

❑ 74. Are you cross merchandising on a regular basis?

❑ 75. Do you use signs to cross merchandise?

❑ 76. Do you suggestion-sell on your signs, such as "Don't forget batteries" when someone buys a flashlight?

Endcaps

❑ 77. How many endcaps do you have?

❑ 78. How often do you change the products on those endcaps?

❑ 79. Do you have a regular schedule of planned endcaps?

❑ 80. Are your endcaps usually sale products or regular-priced items?

❑ 81. Do you cross-merchandise your endcaps?

❑ 82. Knowing that moving merchandise from a side gondola to an endcap will increase sales—do you know by how much in your store?

❑ 83. Did you know that by moving merchandise from a side gondola to an endcap and using a feature/benefit sign, you can increase sales even more?

❑ 84. Do you use uniform, high-impact signs on all your endcaps?

❏ 85. Have you measured the impact of endcaps featuring a single dominant product?

❏ 86. If your endcaps are multi-item, are they related products and clearly signed?

Power Aisles

❏ 87. Do you regularly review the merchandise and signing plans for your power aisle?

❏ 88. Do you make use of stack displays?

❏ 89. Do you cross-merchandise with stack displays?

❏ 90. How are your stack displays signed?

❏ 91. What kind of merchandising do you use at the entrance of your store?

❏ 92. What kind of signs do you use at the entrance?

Dump Bins

❏ 93. Do you use dump bins on a regular, planned basis?

❏ 94. How are your dump bins signed?

❏ 95. Do you have a plan or process to use dump bins for cross-merchandising opportunities in your store?

"One of the biggest wastes of money is the grocery store banner in the window, announcing the week's specials. It all started back in the 1930's when stores needed to stop traffic with window signs. Now, most grocery stores have large parking lots. By the time the customer sees the sign, he or she has already made a decision to stop there. Are you still doing things that don't make sense?"

—Krag Swartz,
Food Marketing Manager

Employees

❏ 96. Do your sales people know as much about your merchandise as you do?

❏ 97. Do your employees know your important store policies and services?

❏ 98. Do your employees seem to be as concerned about your store's image or signing as you are?

❏ 99. Are your sales representatives able to help every customer? ◆

Glossary of Terms

Adjacency In retail store planning, the placement of like departments together or conveniently near each other—adjacent to each other. The study and planning of store layout can be called "adjacencies."

Alphanumeric A simple filing system using a combination of alphabet and numbers.

Bar code A system whereby numbers are translated into bars of different lengths, which can be scanned electronically. Most retail merchandise in the U.S.A. today is bar coded for scanning and automatic price lookup at the checkout or service station.

Basics In retail apparel, it is basic fashion merchandise which does not change shape, year after year. It probably will change in color, from season to season and year to year. T-shirts, turtleneck tops, pull-on pants are examples of basics.

Brand name A recognizable label on merchandise. A name desired by the general public or a specific customer group because the manufacturer has successfully invested in advertising to establish the "brand."

Benefit An advertising or signing copy claim which is customer-oriented. It answers questions such as: "What benefit is this item to the customer?" "What need or desire will this item satisfy?"

Checkout In self-service stores, the area where employees are stationed, with computer terminals, to "ring up" each item and bag it, and where the customer pays for the purchases. Usually located by the main store exit.

Combination signing Creating a sign which may list individual pieces of a setting or logical grouping, and giving a price for the total. Examples: sound systems or computer systems which have several interrelated parts. Each part may be priced separately; a combination sign would give the cost for the total system. It is a customer-service idea which has not been exploited well by retailers.

Commodity Any item of merchandise which is used regularly and disposed of, thus making regular repurchasing necessary. High commodity items are purchased so frequently, the customer has a good idea of the best price, or the last price paid for the item. Examples: toilet paper, disposable diapers, milk, margarine, razor blades, paper towels.

Competitor-reactive A philosophy of advertising and signing which is based on a store's competition (usually a larger business). A store will show competitors' ads and prices, and offer a comparison of its own prices. It depends on competitors' advertising for pricing credibility.

Co-op 1. a group of like stores or manufacturers who have agreed to combine marketing efforts, i.e., a dairy co-op. 2. an advertising agreement between vendor and retailer to pay for an advertisement or special promotion. Vendor support for such advertising or promotion is called "vendor co-op."

Cross-aisle merchandising A relatively new way to present merchandise. Previously, merchandise was placed on two sides of one gondola—the customer had to walk around the gondola or stack of shelves in order to see all the offerings and find what he or she wanted. Cross-aisle merchandising tries to put the merchandise on the adjacent sides of two gondolas, so the customer is standing with the department's offering on both sides—much easier to shop.

Customer count A method of counting how many customers visited a store in a day, week or month. Discounters with checklanes use each transaction as a "customer." Department stores where customers might make several individual purchases on one trip will use literal "counters"—people stationed at the doors to count everyone who enters or exits.

DIY Acronym for "Do It Yourself" and the retailers who sell merchandise for home repair and rejuvenation projects.

Demographics Basic analysis of a population or customer base: age, income, home or car ownership, education, marital status, number of children in home.

Destination purchase A unique, usually higher-price purchase which the customer wants to make, and will travel farther to make. The customer can also comparison shop several stores for this purchase. Examples: winter coats, electronic equipment, cars, lawnmowers, designer clothing, a very special cut of meat.

Digital type Type, such as you are reading here, which is programmed in electronic or scannable equipment, not cast in metal as the original type was. Type that can be manipulated, via computer, to become larger, smaller, wider, etc.

Dump bins Bins, buckets or receptacles in which small merchandise items can be "dumped" instead of being in tidy rows on a shelf. Soap, film, any large amount of similar product can be put in a dump bin and with proper signing, experience increased sales. Best used with a single commodity.

EDL Acronym for "Every Day Low," a pricing strategy where the store rarely has sales or promotional events, but advertises its everyday low prices.

Endcap The end of a gondola or stretch of merchandise. It usually faces an aisle and thus has greater exposure to customers. Moving merchandise from a shelf on a gondola to an endcap can increase sales. With added benefit and price signing, sales can increase significantly.

Everyday low See EDL above.

Face Refers to various styles of type and their weight and design. A "light" face has thin vertical strokes; a "bold" face has thick vertical strokes; an "italic" face tilts forward at the top.

Facings The amount of any one product which will be put on the shelf to face the customer. A single row, forward to back, of one product is one facing. Two rows are two facings, etc. A product with five "flavors" would have at least five facings. The best-selling flavor might have two facings by itself.

Fashion forward Merchandise which is very new looking—the cutting edge of fashion. Apparel which appeals to a small group of people who like experimental dressing or are very aware of fashion trends.

Focus group A research tool using a specially selected cross-section of people to talk about a subject. A trained leader presents the subject to the group, pursues its ideas and makes sure everyone participates. These conversations are recorded and sometimes videotaped. In many cases, observers can watch. Participants are screened to be potential customers, current or disenchanted customers, etc. Using two or more focus groups, each with different attitudes, to discuss the same subject can be very enlightening.

Font An alphabet of type in a certain style. Each set of a typestyle is called a "font." When type was cast in metal, it meant style and size. With electronic type equipment where size is adjustable, it simply means style.

Format A style of presenting visual material. In signing, the placement of copy and prices, and the size of the type for each. A pre-selected grid into which information can be programmed.

Gondola A freestanding base with center support and shelves on both sides and ends (endcaps). Usually 12 or 16 feet long and 5 feet high. Shelves are adjustable and can be replaced with bins, slanting shelves, pegboard according to the limits of the merchandise to be presented. A basic unit of merchandise presentation in most retail stores.

Gross margin Gross profit. In dollars, the difference between the retailer's selling price and what the retailer paid the manufacturer or vendor. It does not include cost of overhead, delivery, etc.

High service Stores with an adequate amount of employees to personally relate to customers and help them make buying decisions. These stores will also furnish informative signing to help customers make buying decisions. Sometimes relates to merchandise which must have high service in order to be sold. Examples: complicated products such as electronic or sound equipment; equipment which may need instruction, such as lawnmowers; expensive merchandise such as jewelry.

Impulse purchase An item bought by the customer while in the store, which the customer did not come to the store intending to buy. Many retailers advertise "loss leaders" or items on which they do not make any money, in order to get people into their stores. They depend upon impulse purchases for their profit. Increasing impulse purchases is the objective of good signing and presentation.

Independent retailer A store or small chain which is privately owned and is not part of a chain or publicly owned. May belong to a cooperative, be a franchise or participate in a buying group.

Irregular Merchandise which has a tiny flaw and has not passed manufacturer's quality control. The flaw may be imperceptible to the customer. However, any sale of irregular merchandise should be clearly labeled, signed and advertised as such.

Knockdown "KD"—simple inexpensive furniture that is sold "knocked down" in pieces to fit a package. The customer assembles the piece at home.

Knock-off A copy. Taking a successful item and having it made cheaper. Originally a term for apparel, where an expensive dress or outfit was purchased by a manufacturer and its designers would work to create the identical-looking dress at a much lower price. Now can be any item, apparel to hardware.

Landscape A sign which is horizontal. A typical "landscape" sign size of 7 x 11″ would be 7 inches high and 11 inches wide.

Layout The graphic contribution to an ad or sign. The placement of a headline, copy and price—sometimes an illustration. The size and type style of the various components.

List price The manufacturer's suggested retail price. The price which the manufacturer has printed on an attached price tag, label or package. The price as listed in a manufacturer's catalog.

Logo A company's signature. A company's official name, set in a unique type, color and/or graphic style so as to set it apart and be not only recognizable but memorable to the customer.

Markdown A reduction in the selling price of an item. A "sale" is a temporary markdown in price; a "clearance" is a permanent markdown.

Mission A written statement of a business' purpose. A mission statement summarizes what the company plans to do in order to be successful. It considers such things as level of quality, price range, merchandise or service assortment, level of service to the customer and the customer profile. As a company grows and more people are making decisions, a mission statement acts as a decision guide for all employees.

Planogram A diagram, sketch or photograph which shows what merchandise to place where on a gondola or wall in a store. It is necessary to make sure that merchandise is presented in an orderly and logical way, to make it easier for the customer to find what he or she is looking for. More sophisticated planograms are computer driven to achieve the most profitable arrangement, and/or the most efficient way to stay in stock on all items.

Platform A base of wood, brick or simple carpet on which bulky merchandise is stacked and signed. Excellent presentation strategy for seasonal merchandise. Traditional method of presenting barbecue grills, artificial Christmas trees, fertilizer.

PLU Acronym for Price Look Up systems, which electronically scan a product's bar code and automatically enter the correct price in the terminal. Can be programmed to give the temporary sale price. This technology not only saves time at the checkout, it saves pricing every item in the store, and re-pricing that item during a sale period. It also allows the store to control inventory, since every transaction is recorded accurately.

Portrait Is the adjective description of a vertical sign. A typical 7 x 11″ sign is "portrait" style when it is 7″ wide and 11″ high.

POP Point of Purchase. The spot where customer meets product, and a sign at that point is called a POP (point of purchase) sign.

POS Point of Sale. Where the customer pays for the merchandise. Computer terminals to handle the sales transactions are called POS terminals.

Pre-print An advertising message printed by the advertiser and delivered to the newspaper, to be inserted in a day's edition. Can be a single sheet but usually is 12 to 16 pages. Can be full newspaper size, half newspaper size or smaller. Usually four-color photography or art.

Price coordinator A retail store employee designated to maintain proper prices on all merchandise, advertised or regular. This person handles or supervises any price change, making sure signing is accurate, individual item pricing is changed, if necessary, and that the price look-up program is coordinated with the changes.

Price points Specific "markers" of price in a store. For instance, 99¢ price endings may be a "sale price point" for department stores yet indicate a regular price in discount stores. 00¢ or even numbers may be a clearance "price point" for some stores. This term may also refer to the lowest price offered in a specific department, i.e., its opening price point. "Magic" price points are price barriers in the minds of customers. "Under $10.00" is perceived as being significantly lower in price than "Over $10.00" even if the amount under or above is minimal. People will pay "Up to xx." Magic price points are 5, 10, 20, 25 and 100 dollars.

Private label A label that is managed by the individual store or chain and sold only by that store or chain. It can have the store's name, or have a separate identity which can appear to be a national brand but isn't. Some manufacturers specialize in providing private label merchandise to retailers. Some stores position their private label as equal to national brands but less expensive. Others position their private label as more expensive and higher quality. Many stores are rejuvenating their private label programs in order to develop unique products.

Promotional A retail strategy that depends upon advertising sales (reduced prices on specific merchandise) on a regular basis. Everyday prices may be a bit higher in order to offset the amount of off-price sales. Prices can be low because of the enormous volume of customer traffic generated by the advertising.

Racetrack A retail term for the main aisle which frequently circles a store. Usually a wider aisle, with checkout terminals at the entrance/exit.

RAMA Retail Advertising and Marketing Association, located in Chicago, which sponsors an annual RAC (Retail Advertising Conference), several other conferences, the Retail Hall of Fame and other awards of recognition in the retail industry.

Rainchecks When a store runs out of sale merchandise, the store can promise a disappointed customer that the customer will get the sale price when the merchandise is again available. The customer's form which promises the sale price is called a "raincheck." In some states, rainchecks are mandatory.

Reverse A typesetting term, whereby the type is white on a dark background—the reverse of typical type which is dark on white background.

"Ring" Retail term for a transaction. Cash registers used to ring as the total was calculated, thus the term for increasing the individual customer transaction was "increasing the ring." Computer terminals don't ring, but the term persists.

Sampling Offering a free tasting of a product to customers in a grocery store. A demonstrator will prepare the food and offer it, next to a display of the product which may have a special low price. Can be a trial-size handout, to introduce a new product.

Sans serif A description of type face which does not have any cross strokes at the end of the letters. Traditional type faces have serifs. Many contemporary type faces are sans serif. Helvetica is a good example.

Scaleable A type system which can make type larger or smaller yet stay in proportion. "Fat" or thick parts of a letter need to be scaled down as the type size increases, otherwise the type becomes overbearing.

Scanning Using an electronic beam to pass over a series of bars and interpret the information: usually item description and price. Refers to retailers' price lookup systems at checkout desks. Bar codes are scanned and the price is automatically established. See PLU.

Seasonal Retailers' description of merchandise that has a short selling period. Examples are bedding plants, fertilizer and weed controllers in northern U.S.A., Christmas trees and giftwrap.

Serif See sans serif.

Software The programs which run on computer hardware.

Special application computer Hardware and software designed to solve a unique need. Can do one thing extremely well, simply and inexpensively.

Template A guide to insure the final shape and arrangement. A term used by Insignia Sign Systems for its signing guides.

Thermal paper Paper which is heat sensitive. Used in computer applications because of the need for high speed.

Trend A shift in the desirability of a product by the general public. Usually defines a product becoming more desirable. Can define an attitude, as in the public's general trend to be more concerned about ecology and willing to recycle.

Turnover A term for how often inventory is sold and replaced. Each replacement is a "turn." A high turn is desirable, in order to increase sales per square foot. Merchandise which does not turn drags down profits — takes space and inventory dollars without getting sales and profits.

Typefaces The various designs of type available. Each design is a "face."

Typography The setting and arrangement of various typefaces which is a special graphics art.

Typestyles See typeface. There are many styles of type—from old Gothic associated with old Bibles, to contemporary sans serif and extremely light styles. Each face has its own style.

Unit pricing A secondary price explanation, usually for food products. The grocer indicates the price for the bottle or package—and then must indicate the corresponding price per ounce or unit. Allows easy comparison shopping, since every price has been reduced to a common unit cost.

Vendor A business which sells to retailers. A manufacturer, wholesaler or one of their representatives could be called a "vendor." Advertising, special promotions or displays which are underwritten by a manufacturer, etc., are called "vendor paid."

Notes

_____

_____

_____

_____

_____

_____

_____

_____

_____

_____

_____

_____

_____

_____

_____

_____

_____

_____

_____

_____

_____

_____

_____

_____

Notes

Notes

Notes